Praise

'*The Human Touch* is a beautifully written self-growth book. Sukaiyna offers insightful concepts and questions that encourage fresh perspectives on our worldviews and coping mechanisms. Highlights include the mirror, untangling, TOUCH and Branch methods, which creatively promote personal growth and improve our collective well-being.'
— **Paul Rashid MD**, Psychiatrist and Author of *Recovery Revolution: A Social Blueprint for Optimal Mental Health*, United States of America

'Sit back. Trust the silence and get ready for a love journey. Release the triggers, hold up a mirror, say what you mean and walk through Ayden's garden to a place of serenity picking flowers of wisdom along the way. You will emerge at peace, joyous and free. A must read, and not only once!'
— **Nanda Shaheen PhD**, UK

'So well written and resonates! Profound yet easy to read and remarkably relatable. I felt good just reading it. Imagine how I'm feeling while I'm digging a little deeper and doing some of the work/exercises. I highly recommend you give it a try.'
— **Waël Kabbani**, award-winning Songwriter, Film Director/Producer and Storyteller (Iambic Dream Films), from Syria and Saudi Arabia, living in Canada and Czech Republic

'*The Human TOUCH* is an invitation to reflect on the connections that unite us across cultures, experiences and borders. It is a testament to a life lived with open eyes and an open heart, encouraging us all to seek understanding in a complex world.'
— **Fritz Straub**, CEO, Deutsche Werkstätten Hellerau, Dresden, Germany

'A beautifully written guide to untangling the complexities of the human spirit, *The Human TOUCH* provides actionable tools for growth and connection. This book is a true gift for those ready to transform their lives.'
— **Nao Stanton**, best-selling Author, from Japan, living in Hawaii, USA

'From Socrates to Carl Jung and those universal axioms that boast a higher consciousness in us, this book needs to be approached with caution, for it carries its scholar to worlds fully unexpected. It is a universal manual to a higher living that is as necessary as water is to life. Yet, this exercise is only for those who desire, not for those who just wish.'
— **Dimitri Andritsoyannis**, Private Equity, from Greece, living between Athens, Greece and New York, USA

'Be prepared to be taken on a journey of self-enlightenment. *The Human TOUCH* unlocks the magic of the human soul and sheds a spotlight on how we can use our powers from within to become

the best version of ourselves and positively impact the lives of those around us.'
— **Joanna Lange**, Founder and Owner of LuxemotionsbyLange, from Northern Ireland, living in Germany

'*The Human TOUCH* is a heartfelt exploration of self-awareness and human connection. Suki masterfully blends reflection, empathy and actionable insights, offering readers a pathway to inner harmony and meaningful relationships. A truly transformative read for anyone seeking clarity and balance in life.'
— **Manuel Greiner**, CEO and Co-Owner, PIEGA, Zurich, Switzerland

'Sukaiyna's guidance in *The Human TOUCH* is practical, her wisdom profound and her tools invaluable. Even after years of self-reflection, her gentle approach unpeels layers of limiting thoughts and habits, making profound concepts both accessible and actionable. If you're ready for true transformation, this is the book for you!'
— **Artemis Doupa**, award-winning Entrepreneur and best-selling Author, from Greece, living in London, United Kingdom

'In our own quest to self-discovery this book is a smart reflection on what we already should know, but need a consistent reminder on. A brilliant eye

opener and a journey back to our forgotten human condition; a guidebook to our deeper selves.'
— **Nihat Tanfer**, Tanfer Group, Istanbul, Turkey

'*The Human TOUCH: A Mirror for Self-Reflection* by Sukaiyna Gokal offers a transformative approach to personal growth. It simplifies complex concepts, promoting self-accountability and empathetic communication. This insightful guide enhances self-awareness and relationships, making it a must-read for anyone seeking deeper understanding. Highly recommended!'
— **Rima Ariss**, Managing Director, TellGngr. online, Beirut, Lebanon

'This book is an excellent portal into understanding key concepts of life and gives really interesting insights into strategies to self-reflect and grow as a person. *The Human TOUCH* by Sukaiyna Gokal is an exceptional novel for advising people by deeply explaining the secrets of evolving as a person by understanding the past and changing for the future.'
— **Kayan Defouni**, Student, age 14, from Egypt, living in United Arab Emirates

'*The Human TOUCH* is the epitome of inner work. If you are serious about diving deeper within and embarking on the transformative journey of self-discovery, this is the book for you. It gently

guides you into your inner world, helping you ascend, align and elevate with grace.'
— **Salina Taqi**, yoga instructor and energy healer @breathewithsalina from Pakistan, living in United Arab Emirates

'Filming video episodes with Sukaiyna about the transformative tools in this book was an emotional journey that deeply touched me. This book feels like revisiting those heartfelt moments.

'If its wisdom were universally implemented, we would inhabit the most peaceful corner of the universe.'
— **Samir Kayal**, Filmmaker, from Lebanon, living in the GCC

'*The Human TOUCH* reflects the ancient wisdom urging us not to conform to the patterns of our generation, but to transform ourselves through a renewed way of thinking. It inspires us to embrace humility, selflessness and love, fostering profound personal and relational growth.
— **Aji John**, Stretch and Relax Coach, Kochi, India

The threads of unity are further connected at the end of the book in the section, Celebrating *The Human TOUCH*.

I didn't know I wasn't until I was...

THE HUMAN
TOUCH

Tolerance *Openness* *Unity* *Collaboration* *Harmony*

A MIRROR FOR SELF-REFLECTION

SUKAIYNA GOKAL

R^ethink

First published in Great Britain in 2025
by Rethink Press (www.rethinkpress.com)

© Copyright Sukaiyna Gokal

All rights reserved. No part of this publication may be reproduced, stored in or introduced into a retrieval system, or transmitted, in any form, or by any means (electronic, mechanical, photocopying, recording or otherwise) without the prior written permission of the publisher.

The right of Sukaiyna Gokal to be identified as the author of this work has been asserted by her in accordance with the Copyright, Designs and Patents Act 1988.

This book is sold subject to the condition that it shall not, by way of trade or otherwise, be lent, resold, hired out, or otherwise circulated without the publisher's prior consent in any form of binding or cover other than that in which it is published and without a similar condition including this condition being imposed on the subsequent purchaser.

Dedicated to

Adil, my precious anchor
Ayden, my magical kite
&
TNT, my scintillating soul sister

Contents

Foreword	**1**
Prologue	**9**
Introduction	**11**
PART ONE The Vision	**19**
The Human TOUCH	**21**
Seed 1 – Tolerance	23
Seed 2 – Openness	25
Seed 3 – Unity	26
Seed 4 – Collaboration	27
Seed 5 – Harmony	29
Transition From Part One To Part Two	**31**
PART TWO Enter The Garden: You With You	**35**
Impressionism – Perceptions And Illusions	**37**
Branch 1.1 – Misconceptions and limiting beliefs	37
Branch 1.2 – Understanding the beautiful complexity of the human being	42

Branch 1.3 – The irony of the importance of the 'I' — 47

The Greenhouse – Self-Reflection — 53
Branch 2.1 – What were the contexts during my childhood? — 54
Branch 2.2 – What impact does my childhood have on my today? — 58
Branch 2.3 – By questioning my childhood beliefs, I see myself differently — 62

The Season Of Your Heart – Self-Awareness And Self-Knowledge — 67
Branch 3.1 – Observing the pattern of my thoughts — 67
Branch 3.2 – A close look in the mirror — 72
Branch 3.3 – The renovation of my thoughts — 77

Mother Nature Vs. Mother Nurture – Self-Accountability — 83
Branch 4.1 – The correlation of heart, mind, body and soul — 83
Branch 4.2 – A deep breath of forgiveness while releasing triggers — 89
Branch 4.3 – Looking at my definition of harmony — 93

Waltzing In The Wilderness Or In Wisdom – Responsibility — 99
Branch 5.1 – The importance of graceful communication — 99
Branch 5.2 – The kaleidoscope of non-verbal communication — 104

Branch 5.3 – The kaleidoscope of verbal communication ... 108

Pruning Of The Tree – Creating Your Vision ... 115
Branch 6.1 – The beauty of self-trust ... 115
Branch 6.2 – Defining my purpose ... 120
Branch 6.3 – Surrender and flow ... 125

Transition From Part Two To Part Three ... 131

PART THREE Looking at the I with a Deeper Eye: You With Others ... 133

Untangling Perspectives And Reframing Perceptions ... 135
Branch 1.1 – The clay half-baked or overcooked ... 135
Branch 1.2 – Dancing with discomfort ... 140
Branch 1.3 – Secrets and sacrifices ... 144

The Desire To Be Deserving ... 149
Branch 2.1 – The rose and the thorn ... 149
Branch 2.2 – The juxtaposition of joy vs. jealousy ... 154
Branch 2.3 – The ability to forgive everything, knowing it takes two to tango ... 158

The Constant Evolution Of Our Person ... 163
Branch 3.1 – The flexibility of my impressions ... 163
Branch 3.2 – Is a mistake a misery or a miracle? ... 168
Branch 3.3 – Retrospect is respect for what was ... 172

The Context Of My Childhood   **177**
    Branch 4.1 – Looking for patterns that
    I didn't realise were guiding my journey   177
    Branch 4.2 – Calling a spade 'a spade'   181
    Branch 4.3 – Perfecting my prism   185

Regal Responsibilities, Majestic Mindsets
And Embracing Empathy   **189**
    Branch 5.1 – The magic of motherhood   189
    Branch 5.2 – Releasing the riot of resentment   195
    Branch 5.3 – Roles and responsibilities   200

Meditation And Mediation   **205**
    Branch 6.1 – Nullifying the negative
    narrative   205
    Branch 6.2 – Disclosure with disclaimer   209
    Branch 6.3 – The roller coaster towards
    repair and restoration   214

Conclusion   **219**
    The Guiding principles of
    The Human Touch   219
    The Muse – Stepping from contemplation
    into action   221
    Meditation   223

Epilogue   **225**

Celebrating *The Human TOUCH*   **227**

Resources   **243**
    Self-reflective tools   243
    The Muse Journal   246

Garden of Ayden Meditation	246
Garden of Ayden Radio Playlist	246
Acknowledgements	**247**
The Author	**249**

Foreword

There are many books that promise to guide you on a journey of self-discovery, but few that actually share a magnificent, well-trodden and tested path of enlightenment and fulfillment.

Enter my dear friend Sukaiyna Gokal, who's lifetime work brings you *The Human Touch* – her experience and professionalism qualifies her uniquely to connect with you from your very core.

Writing a foreword for this book is not just a privilege but a heartfelt honour, as it allows me to celebrate the extraordinary individual behind its pages. Sukaiyna's mission in life has been to open the minds of those around her to the endless possibilities that we all possess and control, be it her clients, her friends or the wider community.

By bringing us on a pragmatic and common-sense journey to help find inner peace, she encourages us to expand our universe, to explore and find tolerance, understanding and harmony.

I've been lucky to know Sukaiyna for several years and, on the outset, one might wonder how and why we've become such dear friends. Her calm, embracing demeanour could well have clashed with my sometimes brash and hectic disposition. My pace of life could sometimes be compared to the speed-free part of the autobahn, whereby hers is the steady garden path full of endless discoveries, scents and sights and visions beyond the imagination. Yet we clicked, and while we will never be carbon copies of each other, we do complement each other in that grand space that embraces differences. A space not everyone gets comfortable in, but one worth exploring.

Her Garden of Ayden programme, the long-established guide to help you find inner peace and harmony, reminds us that we all need to take the time to be present for ourselves and to get to know ourselves a little bit better. Think from inside out, or outside in, where's your best perspective?

She reminds us that we need to occasionally slow down, stand back, take a bird's eye view and pull back

FOREWORD

from the stresses of our daily lives. By doing so with greater awareness and regularity, we will soon find the space that will help us carve different paths through physical and metaphorical landscapes and reflect on the beauty around us. This book is more than just a good read and a working guide; it is a testament to Sukaiyna's unwavering dedication to helping others find contentment and greater meaning in their lives.

This book is a gift to us all, it's designed to help guide us toward a place of greater understanding and peace of mind. It's an invitation to embark on a journey of self-discovery; to hold up a mirror to our souls, revealing truths we may have ignored or buried, and perhaps some we should have buried long ago.

Through its pages, she knows how to lead from the head and from the heart and tells us why we must forever trust our intuition. She takes us by the hand and guides us through the complexities of our inner world with the same loving care, compassion and wisdom she has brought to countless lives. This is not the result of a single moment or epiphany on her behalf; it's the culmination of a lifelong commitment of learning, growing and understanding about what it means to truly live life in balance. It's something I know we all ultimately strive for.

She has drawn from diverse experiences, cultures and philosophies and has managed to weave these learnings into a unique tapestry of wisdom that resonates universally. *The Human Touch* is not just a book, it's a practical guide full of reflections and exercises to help us chart our progress and transform our thoughts and actions into a way of life.

She observes how we are all on the same journey in this world, no matter our views, ethnicity or social standing, but each one of us is at a different stage in our evolution. There's so much we can learn from each other along the way, but we often get stuck, overwhelmed and downright confused. *The Human Touch* reminds us of the power within and of our ability to solve what sometimes looks like an unfathomable hurdle. When we stop to think and analyse, the seeds that we germinate so often deliver the right solutions and we can even surprise ourselves.

More importantly, we can all help each other with the shared wisdom of our experiences and spread insight into the complexity of our perspectives and diverse eclectic knowledge. But the starting point must be understanding, acceptance and trust of self; traits we often fail to appreciate.

It is the culmination of her own inquisitive and challenging experiences through life – alongside a refreshing dollop of introspection and a container load of research – that curated Garden of Ayden, a company she founded in 2012. She did this to be of service to others and to honour the life-long company of her young son, the representation of hope for the future.

FOREWORD

She has spent the past decade assisting troubled and often just curious souls, untangle themselves from the chaos of life, to find truth in the simplest manner, with as little noise as possible. Who would have thought it could be so easy.

This book is not about quick fixes or surface-level solutions. It is about exceptional transformation, the kind that begins within and radiates outward, affecting our relationships, our communities and ultimately the world.

It challenges us to confront our fears, insecurities and biases, but it does so with gentleness and empathy. Each chapter is a step forward, a piece of the puzzle that, when assembled, reveals a picture of a life lived with intention, clarity and peace.

One of the most revealing and remarkable aspects of her work is her ability to make the abstract tangible. Concepts like harmony, contentment and understanding can often feel elusive, but she breaks them down in ways that are accessible and actionable for every one of us.

Her teachings are rooted in authenticity. She does not merely preach these principles; she lives them, and her life is a testament to the power and practice of these ideas. Those who have worked with her or have had the pleasure of being in her company know only too well her joyful and gracious impact.

This book also serves as a reminder of the interconnectedness of our lives. As she so beautifully illustrates, finding peace within ourselves is not a solitary endeavour; it is a ripple that extends outward, touching everyone and everything we encounter. By healing ourselves, we contribute to the healing of our families, communities and the world at large. This is perhaps one of the most powerful messages of the book: that our individual journeys are part of a greater collective story and really do have the power to change lives.

As you turn the pages, you will find yourself pausing, reflecting and sometimes even questioning. That's all part of the design, think, pause, rethink and sometimes reset. Growth often begins with discomfort, and the questions she poses are not meant to challenge just for the sake of the challenge, but to lead us to a place of greater insight and understanding. She encourages us to be honest with ourselves, to hold a mirror to our souls, to embrace our imperfections, and to see them not as obstacles but as learnings and opportunities for growth.

Too often our chaotic world is driven by division, unrest, and a sense of disconnection. Responsible people not always taking responsibility. In such times, the lessons of this book are more urgent and relevant than ever, reminding us that peace is not something we can wait around for or seek outside ourselves; it is something we can create, cultivate and share. Even if it's just within ourselves, our families and friends and communities.

FOREWORD

The journey of *The Human Touch* will help transform the life of the reader, but it will also contribute to a more harmonious and compassionate environment. Embrace it and read it with an open heart and an open mind, and you will find within its pages the tools, insights and inspiration to create a life of greater calm and contentment.

To my dear friend Sukaiyna, thank you for being a guiding light, not just for me but for everyone who has been fortunate enough to cross your path. Your work is a testament to the power of kindness, patience and unwavering faith in the human spirit. This book is a reflection of all that you are and all that you have given to those close to you and to the wider world. It is a legacy that will continue to engage, inform, educate and hopefully inspire generations to come.

To the reader, in the nicest possible way, prepare to be confronted, to be challenged and to be charged with a call for change. Your reward will be a clearer understanding of who you are from inside out and that clarity will lead to the harmony and acceptance you crave to make your life richer.

For this we thank you Sukaiyna and acknowledge your life and work as a testament to the transformative power of love, wisdom, and compassion.

Eithne Treanor, Founder and CEO, E Treanor Media, from Ireland, living in Dubai

Prologue

Sukaiyna Gokal has built bridges for us to cross, leading us into the sanctuary of her garden—a place alive with the seeds she has lovingly planted for human growth and transformation. In this sacred space, she invites us to pause, to explore the depths of our inner selves, and to gather the strength to meet the challenges of the outer world with authenticity and grace.

Through her journey, Sukaiyna has courageously reflected on her inner being, sharing her insights with the world of the here and now. Her message is clear and profound: Know yourself so that you can truly know others. Love yourself so that you can deeply love others. Be yourself. Laugh at yourself. Be authentic and genuine, for only then can you face the trials of life and the complexities of the world with resilience and clarity.

Her wisdom inspires us to embrace vulnerability and self-discovery as tools for growth. By showing us how to find joy in being truly ourselves, she lights a path for us to follow. Sukaiyna is not just a teacher of life's lessons; she is a living testament to the power of authenticity, a beacon of hope, and, above all, a delight to us all.

Bob Shaheen

Introduction

We are all on the same journey of this delicate life and each one of us is at a different station in our evolution. We can help each other with both the wisdom of our experiences and insight into the complex light of our individual perspectives and eclectic knowledge. We all have a story and narratives that are of value, which may breed self-reflection and inner growth for others. The gems that we germinate within are fascinating and often even surprise ourselves.

It is the privilege of my challenging experiences through life – alongside a dollop of introspection and a container load of study – that curated Garden of Ayden, a company I founded in 2012 to be of service to others, to assist them to untangle themselves to find their truths in the simplest manner, with little noise. There is always a defining moment, turning point or epiphany that alters our course to release the fountain of what we have buried within. I say this with deep faith and respect, knowing that you too have so many hidden gems within yourself, whether you have acknowledged it to yourself as yet or not.

My epiphany was the birth of my son, Ayden. I had already mourned the fact that I would never have children. Serendipitously, during my fortieth year, I was blessed that he chose me to be his mother. What was born within me was a burning desire to ensure he never suffer any of my pains. I visualised the metaphor of sandpaper dust cleansing my heart to ensure it became free of any hurt, to be healed of any inner wounds, knowing that as parents it is our internal state of peace and well-being that provides the map for our children's journeys. This became my labour of love, seeking truth and authenticity, which resulted in the birth of Garden of Ayden.

I would love to tell you that Ayden's name was sought spiritually, however, I must admit that it was not. My son got his name from my cousin Farah, who suggested the name after seeing a handsome model named Ayden. I looked the name up and was thrilled to learn that it means 'enlightenment'. Calling our platform Garden of Ayden was Ayden's father's idea, which I found brilliant, not knowing at that time that it had such a deep resonance to my journey ahead,

INTRODUCTION

which now, in retrospect, makes perfect sense to me. The reason I mention this is simply to assert that one of my deepest learnings has been the following; when we are open to and follow the signs that are offered to us, we can observe synchronicity effortlessly unfolding our deeply spiritual journey. We are all constantly gifted the signs. When we are open to observe, recognise and nurture them, we unlock all possibilities.

When we polish the diamonds of our souls and surrender ourselves to trusting the light within, we open many dominions of delight, beyond all the pains we have suffered. It took time for me to realise that my humble knowledge and experiences may assist others in recognising, aligning and defining their truths. Hence here I am, respectfully offering you my insight to allow you to polish your own mirrors, experience your own epiphanies and achieve your purpose simply. We all have gems to bring healing to this world, and if you haven't yet, I truly hope you will seek out yours.

We are all unique and special. This journey assisted me in validating my experiences, my courage and my worth. I hope my labour of love will be a catalyst to confirm yours. Should you already be on the journey, I hope this will serve as an endorsement, an inspiration and a reminder to continue to build further.

This is a simple roadmap to untangle perceptions, within a baseline of values we may all agree upon, irrespective of our cultural heritage, gender or religious background. An utterly simple process so that anyone, anywhere may be able to absorb, grasp and be transformed by looking within, while asking themselves the right questions.

Within this book, there are three parts:

Part One, The Vision, is a humble tapestry of the acronym of the human TOUCH in five seeds: tolerance, openness, unity, collaboration and harmony. We visualise the seeds prior to entering the Garden, where we may plant and nurture them.

Part Two, Enter the Garden, is an exploratory mirror for us to journey together effortlessly. Healing is much simpler than we often realise. It guides us to gently look within. It unveils questions, answers of which release any false impressions we may be unconsciously harbouring. It is simple and painless. It relieves any shadows thoroughly, leaving us feeling light-hearted and light-spirited while curating a new meaning to the word 'tranquillity' within us.

It contains six modules, each with three branches. The QR codes at the end of each branch within each module invite you to download a self-reflective tool (SRT) to contemplate online and fill in digitally, or to print, if you enjoy putting pen to paper as I do.[1] These tools serve as impact measures, which you may review

---

1   The self-reflective tools are available in eighteen languages.

and complete again (even repeatedly at each stage of your journey) upon completion of the book. This will validate the polishing process of your mirror. It's wonderfully useful and gratifying, as measuring our inner changes can be so perplexing. It is worth even beginning the book again once you have completed it, as it continues to take you deeper each time you read it. It's so interesting how in reading the same words we stretch and expand even further.

Coping is the measure of how large our vessel is to contain everything that happens to us. Imagine if our vessel is the size of a glass – if it overpours, we are unable to breathe. If our vessel is the size of the ocean, we welcome every new drop with grace. I would like to believe we have a magical talent of achieving this 'vessel growth' when we Enter the Garden.

Enter the Garden has been a class we have been teaching for more than ten years, with many visible proofs of outcomes. This has been the encouragement for this published keepsake. May it impact and help the lives of our global community. May it have the capacity to bring great change to our individual journeys and impact us all collectively.

Part Three, Looking At The I With A Deeper Eye, reflects on our interactions with others. It contains six more modules, again with three branches in each. It's almost like a revolving kaleidoscope after Enter the Garden as it takes you deeper to a finer reframe to complete your perspectives. There are no SRTs in Part Three because they are contained within the beauty of *The Muse*.

In the Conclusion, you will find a link to *The Muse*, which is a gift for you. It is a complete workbook to concretise your learnings, to be downloaded and printed or completed online. It assists in defining a fresh narrative and concise goals going forward.

There is no right and wrong on this journey. We are all in it together.

I would love for this work to be a mirror for you. It contradicts no school of thought; it embraces universal values that we may all agree upon. In case you are curious to learn more, please kindly explore Garden of Ayden, which is a twist on Garden of Eden, a modern-day utopia.

Read this book with an open heart and the following premise: there is a huge difference between our hearts and our emotions. Many a time the emotions that accompany our hearts do not necessarily serve us, hence it is best to let them rest and take a break. We keep the lessons and let go of the stories. This sounds quite unusual, however I invite you to give it a try. Let's forget about the feelings we have about our feelings for a minute.

INTRODUCTION

After unchaining the emotions, we also separate heart and mind. It is the mind that usually chains us to thoughts that eventually victimise us. When we let go of the story, we become free. We simply acknowledge and accept any stories that created who we are. We become grateful. We gain wisdom. We keep moving.

You are not your story, and your story is not you. We are products of our decisions, not of our circumstances. We are born with so much intelligence and yet we tend to feel overwhelmed by doubt as to our capacity. We are as capable as we decide. Any circumstantial trauma endured in time serves as a beautiful gift in how to appreciate the magnitude of the magic and simplicity of bliss.

Ayden means enlightenment, which we define as non-judgement, non-resistance and non-attachment. I sincerely hope you enjoy your journey of enlightenment, contemplating the seeds and bloom of your garden as much as I continue to enjoy mine. I am always available and welcome you, should you wish to reach out.

✉ humantouch@gardenofayden.com

Sending you much love, light and gratitude,

Suki

PART ONE
THE VISION

PART ONE
THE VISION

The Human TOUCH

I didn't know I wasn't until I was.

Can we precisely define anything unless we have experienced it within?

With the internal experience, we may clarify our beliefs with wisdom.

When I began polishing my mirror, I faced millions of mirrors, which didn't help. Discerning my beliefs took many painful years – a curse or a privilege that many cannot afford, be it in time, thick skin, literacy or resources. This is why I now humbly share my process and method with you, as a tool to discern your own beliefs.

Here are some questions to ponder:

- Is there division and fear in our world rather than peace and purpose?
- Does everything feel more disconnected while our world has increased connectivity?
- Has self-accountability been lost to self-interest?
- Has conscientiousness been poisoned by greed?
- Is there more false justification than values that shine bright?
- Has the frequency of our planet reached an all-time low during the most connected era?
- Are we lost in a labyrinth of divided ethics and divine differences?
- Has common sense been manipulated to prey on the ignorant, driving us to believe in and praise falsehoods?
- Do you agree that Man by nature, is inherently selfish and often forgets that this journey is fragile and limited by time?

What we are striving to achieve is an awakening of solidarity and oneness, irrespective of the natural nature of Man, as Man may continuously evolve.

My only wish for you as you read ahead is to befriend the benefit of the doubt. Remain curiously curious to kiss the cynic goodbye, flirt with your triggers and enjoy embracing truths.

I didn't know I wasn't until I was.

This is, of course, after sending your ego on holiday and inviting any old baggage to sit in the sidelines until we Enter the Garden. In the Garden I invite you to play with any demons you may harbour and enjoy untangling the beautiful knots that may be holding space within your precious person.

This first part of the book is a humble tapestry of the acronym of the human TOUCH in five seeds: tolerance, openness, unity, collaboration and harmony. We visualise the following seeds prior to entering the Garden, where we may plant and nurture them.

Seed 1 – Tolerance

Embracing differences and creating bridges rather than borders.

> *Accepting that we are all allowed to be free and we cannot impose our views on others.*

The blueprint of the heart is one we all share yet is etched upon by the context of individual journeys.

How does one define a mirror for all? We leave no room for anything that causes unnecessary issues that feed cognitive biases. We imagine that human beings – even if they may sometimes exhibit bad behaviour – may have the best of intentions. We cannot see intent. Is it possible that someone doing bad things genuinely thinks that they are right in their impressions while remaining unconscious?

Bad behaviour may be corrected; bad intentions require revisiting, repolishing and reawakening.

We polish our own mirror to awaken our deeper intuition to invite self-understanding and witness our true nature without any judgement. Tolerance begins with us. Ignorance can never be an excuse for intolerance.

With our intuition polished and awake, errors present within our thinking or actions have the ability to come to the surface. They become simple observations that guide us towards becoming graceful in maintaining boundaries, exercising caution and embracing our freedom.

Seed 2 – Openness

Being accepting of ideas, views and opinions and being ready to learn.

Our differences may complement us rather than divide us.

Think of someone that triggers you. What happens inside of you?

From here on, when you see a person that triggers you coming towards you, smile and say, 'Here comes my teacher!' It will change the game.

Be open to understand yourself rather than focusing on your distaste and dislike of the other. Openness is about the willingness to interact without judgement. Your judgement of others speaks more about *you* than of them. We never know if the other is simply misinformed, manipulated or truly ignorant.

To be truly human means to engage wholesomely with anyone that crosses your path. Ask the right questions. What we know for sure is that we don't know, and any presumption to the contrary speaks volumes about our ignorance. Think about the following questions:

- How much of your ego do you bring to any conversation?
- Do you feel a need to be right in what you say?
- Are you honest with your intentions?
- Are you discerning in your communication?
- Is what others see of you truly who you are because you are open?

Seed 3 – Unity

Everyone is included; no one is excluded.

We want to create peace and avoid prejudiced thinking.

A fish cannot climb a tree.

Let's get comfortable with discomfort. Let's challenge ourselves to take the steps that usually scare us and welcome a new and improved cloak of comfort. Let's be vulnerable in identifying our limitations, which may be self-created and self-imposed. They may even be so well manipulated that we are lost within the lies in an illusion of untruths. Dig deeper.

It is about intuition and intention. Has your mind ever convinced yourself of something, yet your intuition nagged at you, then when you decided to ignore your intuition and listen to your mind, you realised it was a mistake? Or did you decide to follow your intuition because you trust yourself deeply and were relieved to realise that you did the right thing?

Let's challenge ourselves to think outside the box and remove any chains and constraints that are limiting our capacity. The freedom is ours to quieten our minds, reframe any school of thought and continue to expand our levels of awareness.

It's only fools who don't change their mind.

Seed 4 – Collaboration

We put our individual differences aside and all work together towards the same goal.

At the root, it is all about how we think and how we act.

Mastery of the individual sadly gets lost when we are all stuck in our own spheres rather than appreciating how many eclectic spheres there are. It challenges collaboration unless we all open our minds to appreciate and validate the diverse collective.

At a beautiful launch of a unique product in an old theatre in Paris, the crowd was buzzing to see and be seen. The scientist who created this magnificent product was unable to translate his awe, his charisma hidden quietly within his mind, sadly lacking the necessary flair to engage his uninspired audience.

The globe is populated by specialists in so many different fields, yet a significant challenge arises from their difficulty in communicating. For instance, how can a scientist truly grasp the nuances of a philosopher's perspective, and how can a ballet dancer appreciate a mathematician's reasoning?

Bridging broader perspectives will enable us to envision and create a world rooted in collaboration and harmony where we sincerely begin to respect the uniqueness of each expertise.

Seed 5 – Harmony

Acceptance, boundaries, respect, unconditional love, protection of humanity and nature.

A father, mother and child visit family friends. The child runs ahead, sees a dog and goes towards it. They cuddle and play, with the father close by. The mother walks in and screams, afraid because she was bitten by a dog as a child. The father looks up in irritation as the child begins to scream, mimicking the unworthy lesson their mother has unconsciously taught them.

We must be discerning in what we force ourselves to absorb, be it unconsciously, manipulatively or purposefully. By nature, we are all loving and harmonious creatures. We need to carefully identify contexts that are driving harmony away from us and us away from harmony. We can iron out wrinkles in a newspaper, so why not from our deeper selves to unveil collective harmony?

A beautiful metaphor: imagine our vision is blurred by all the coloured glass panes of our experiences where the sunlight cannot pierce through to enlighten our hearts. We must dust off and polish some of the coloured glass to reveal crystal clarity for the sunlight to pierce our consciousness and conscientiousness. Then there is light.

Transition From Part One To Part Two

I would like to imagine the five seeds of The Human TOUCH as the Batman signal in the sky that shines a light to challenge us all to deeply awaken and step into our highest and best nature.

Enter the Garden is the simple roadmap to rouse us. It is a gentle unfolding of our person as we look in the mirror and get to know ourselves better, while opening our minds. We contemplate the schools of thought that drive us; we contemplate why, and make shifts to uplift ourselves and those around us.

It's sad to hear people talk about the misery in their lives, in their mindsets, in their couples, in their families and in the world at large. It is baffling that we do not realise that all the resources we need are within us. We have at our disposal simple methods to ease the complexity, invite peace of mind and refine our decision-making skills. May this roadmap bring a widening of perspective and real change.

I have witnessed this magic in my clients and all those that surround me. I am a believer that anything is possible. Let's together elevate the frequency in our world to plant the seeds of hope to bear the fruit of harmony for humanity. There is no reason for anyone to continue to live as a victim within. It necessitates an inner curiosity and thirst for a renewed impression of our own self-worth.

As we now Enter the Garden there is an incredible opportunity to silence the 'no's' and the 'it's impossibles' to reveal your superhero cloak that you will adorn alongside me. One by one, when we each don our cloaks, we will nourish the necessary treasure trove of values we all seek for a safe and peaceful world altogether – and I mean altogether. No one is denied this access; everyone has potential. Remember, it's only fools who don't change their minds, hence we invite the glass ceiling of all possibility.

Sadly, those living in an illusion of darkness may be unaware that this is the case. By shining this light bright and giving the opportunity for all to rekindle their flame without fear, we can each untangle our inner complexity and find internal peace. We all have an inner radar that may be covered in a blanket of unawareness. When we make this effort of entering the garden to polish it, we can become masters of intuitive discernment. This may pave the way for global peace to come naturally.

PART TWO
ENTER THE GARDEN: YOU WITH YOU

PART TWO
ENTER THE GARDEN:
YOU WITH YOU

ENTER THE GARDEN: MODULE 1
Impressionism – Perceptions And Illusions

Purpose: We learn that the world doesn't function the way we think. Your life is defined by you and does not correlate with anyone else's reality. We all see things from a different perspective or through a different lens, which is coloured by our own life experiences. There is no right or wrong; we are each entitled to our own impressions.

Branch 1.1 – Misconceptions and limiting beliefs

Goal: To not believe everything I think, feel, hear and see.

Duality: Freedom in the infinite vs. limitation in ignorant fear.

Epiphany: The only thing I know is that I don't know.

Affirmation: I accept that my reality is not everyone else's reality.

This is a journey of polishing the gems of our minds, hearts and souls. We all belong to this magnificent tapestry of interwoven threads and eclectic colours. My purpose is simply to unify us in a few principles we may all agree upon that may alleviate any potential doubt, discord or disharmony.

Everyone's truth is their own. It seems we cannot play dictator in forcing our truths. We may certainly disagree. When we contemplate from a bird's-eye view, we cannot moderate any generalisation to harmonise all our views. We cannot zoom into and align any common truth as the world stands per se. There will always be *your* truth, *my* truth and a *real* truth. We may only discover the real truth once we shift dimensions where wisdom is the ultimate master. We simply have no choice but to hand the grievances that we don't comprehend over to the unknown to be answered later.

For there to be a genuine peace that surrounds us, we need to admit that we don't know everything, and the only thing we do know for sure is that we don't know. Knowing that to be the case, we can sooner relinquish any battles of wanting to be right, let go of our false impressions and unlearn any old unhelpful concepts that no longer serve us.

IMPRESSIONISM – PERCEPTIONS AND ILLUSIONS

The journey is about unlearning what we may have been slowly brainwashed with or suddenly startled by, while generously granting our impressions the benefit of the doubt, as opposed to coining them as fact.

I realised early on that if the impressions I was holding of or within myself were faulty, no teacher in the world could help me. It became my duty to understand what was real and what was conditioned, and it was daunting. It was almost as if I needed to unlearn everything I held as factual and raise every speck of dust up to the light to reinspect, re-evaluate and revalidate. Sadly, I realised that there were very few of my impressions that I was able to crown proudly in the sunlight as truth; hence, here I am, simply setting the stage for you and your contemplation, not suggesting what beliefs you take away with you.

Let's be mindful of simple perspectives that may alter not only our paths but also our perception of ourselves, others and the world at large. I am not suggesting that there is anything wrong with your thinking – as I said, there is no right or wrong, we are all entitled to our impressions. I am simply offering you a mirror to pause and reflect upon, with the hope of refining and rebalancing anything that may offer you a wider lens of awareness.

My story had carved the unconscious version of myself, which was ready to be scrubbed vigorously and sculpted delicately, while I took distance and began anew with a blank canvas. I invite you to do the same.

While contemplating the canvas of our lives metaphorically, we may become suffocated by so many stories woven together into smudged blotches of paint that are probably not a reliable reflection of our perception. We may be weighed down by so many events we etched so skilfully onto our hearts, we did not realise the extensive storage of baggage that we created. Our feelings that accompanied those events confuse the colours of our tapestry and in turn muddle the experiences we believed we had compartmentalised so carefully. Our cognitive biases thereafter reaffirm our narrative by adding more depth of shadows to our canvas; details and colours of which eventually became naturally muddier and more undefined. Being captivated by our own stories, there is little space for any fresh brushstrokes of sunlight to brighten and lift the dullness of our already weighed-down canvas.

The blank canvas is so refreshing. We reframe the story from scratch from an objective eye. We get to know ourselves better in who we are now, rather than defining ourselves from reflections of our past. We may become well-preserved rather than aged by the definitions that we self-imposed or that were subconsciously gifted to us. We humbly begin afresh.

Imagine if I am wearing shattered glasses with shards of memorabilia that accompany the trail ahead of me.

Everything I look at is distorted and is a complete misrepresentation of the hero within, who has survived many a battle. When I remove the shattered glasses and replace them with pink sparkling frames, my world is enlightened and my eyes brightened. Choice is a freedom we all enjoy.

The child within may hold impressions from the past that are a distorted reflection of our childhood. Imagine the home you grew up in. Returning as an adult, you witness a dramatic dimension change. When contemplating the impact of any traumatic memories that may be still ruminating within, we may reduce them substantially. We loosen the hold they have on us, as we may re-evaluate their dramatic effect. This allows us to question the truths we held onto as facts, to re-examine and re-evaluate. We have every possibility of reframing anything from our past, by shedding the story to invite new horizons.

Are we looking at things inward out or outward in? Allow me to explain. If I am looking at things outward in, it is constant panic, measuring myself via the eyes of how others view me. I am agitated, putting myself constantly under a magnifying glass, measuring my self-worth through my opinion of their opinion. Why do they deserve this credit – and that too a speculated one? Since life is constantly moving and not stagnant, this naturally breeds a lot of unease and is such a waste of precious time and energy.

If I am looking at things inward out, I am structured within, and I challenge myself to rise over and above my expectations of myself. I am my toughest taskmaster yet, being my own best friend. I am measuring myself only against myself. I don't push myself beyond what I am capable of. I am aware that I need balance to be at peace. Everything else fades and silences itself out while I begin to plant and grow the space of an empty and balanced mind focused within.

Contemplate where you are today in this first SRT and return to it after completing the book to measure the internal impact.

Self-Reflective Tool 1.1: The Four Goals of Garden of Ayden, www.gardenofayden.com/ 11thefourgoalsofgardenofayden

Branch 1.2 – Understanding the beautiful complexity of the human being

Goal: To see how many different characteristics people have.

Duality: Knowledgeably humble vs. ignorantly arrogant.

Epiphany: I understand we all perceive and process things differently.

Affirmation: I allow myself to observe with curiosity and an open mind.

As members of our birth family often share so little in common, how may there be the possibility for humanity to align? While you read this, I know you could be of a different gender, age, ethnic background, culture, geography, language, belief system or indoctrination to me. It is certain that there are also genetic, personality, cognitive, emotional and dietary differences as well as dietary intolerances – the list is endless.

May we all allow our similitudes to align us and our differences to complement us while celebrating the variety of blessings, diversity and richness that inhabit our earth. The beauty of our earth contains mountains, deserts, islands, canyons, volcanoes and thousands of types of fruits and vegetables, some of which are rare and unique to certain areas. This exemplifies the rich agricultural heritage and biodiversity of our planet. Millions of different species of animals and around 10,000 species of birds can be classified into various groups depending on their physical characteristics, behaviour and adaptations that allow them to thrive in their respective environments. Thousands of species of fish inhabit different marine environments, from the deep sea to the coral reefs, and can be categorised by their skeletal structure, habitat preferences and feeding habits.

Climates across our globe vary. We adjust and adapt, based upon where we live, where we travel to and the seasons of the year. There are countless types of cuisine which we all enjoy, irrespective of belonging to the culture or not. Beyond this, there are religions and spiritual practices that are not disassociated and spread across the globe. There are educational bodies and philosophies spread across the world as well, which globalisation has afforded us.

The reason I wish to pay respect to the glorious aspects of our splendid earth is, albeit simply, to point out our similarities as human beings. We all have a body, a mind, a heart and a soul. These unite us as human beings. We have been gifted with the abilities to see, hear and feel, as well as think, discern and appreciate. We are gifted with the freedom of choice. We choose what clothes to wear, our routine, who surrounds us and the work we wish to do. There are millions of professions to choose from.

We may welcome tropical travel and culinary curiosity as a natural progression of our cultivation during a well-lived life. Do we also welcome the same curiosity about different types of people? Do we perhaps remain sometimes closed if they do not look or sound like us? If their economical background and status reveals similarity to ours, we may humour them for potential interest or gain. Do we not humour those who are of a different background? Are we truly selfish as a human race or are we open? Do we measure others upon our shattered lens, or do we seek similarities while observing their qualities and appreciating the differences? Are we observing and judging superficially based upon our indoctrination and experiences or are we able to widen our scope? What is it that determines the culture or family we are born into? With this question in mind, how blessed do you feel being born into the heritage that you call your own?

Just as we have so many facets to our world, we have many facets to our minds as well in the way we interpret things. How much time and study have you put into understanding yourself? Do you feel you know yourself well? Is it perhaps your subjectivity that guides you still? We all subconsciously look for safety in what is familiar, be it in attitudes or opinion, and we naturally challenge the unfamiliar.

If I do not make you wrong, you will never be stubborn with me. Hence, let's walk this path together towards alignment and agreement, beyond our conditioning. Let's start by giving the benefit of the doubt to every moment of our day. We release any judgements that come up on autopilot. We engage our blank canvas to create space.

Leaving aside the nuances of culture, language and dialect, we have limitless emotions within the human heart as well as endless possible diseases that unite us in the struggles within the human body.

What is it that may unite us as a species? It cannot be faith because we have so many religions and even sects among them. It cannot be inherited qualities, as a father who is a banker may object to his son wanting to be a drummer and create conflict based upon differences.

There are potentially hundreds of thousands of species of flowers on our planet that coexist peacefully and whose aromas are often blended together and used across the world by global brands to form gorgeous perfumes. The fantastic array of flowers and botanical gardens additionally form colours and textures and create moods to act as muses for fabrics, teas and many other things that are not restricted to culture or ethnicity.

What if we are to return to our blank canvas now and visualise filling our hands with seeds and showering them upon a new secret garden within? Let's recreate a novel theme of our vision of life with a fresh eye.

I leave you with a series of self-reflective questions to deepen your perspectives.

Self-Reflective Tool 1.2: Series of Thought Reflective Questions, www.gardenofayden.com/12seriesofthoughtreflectivequestions

Branch 1.3 – The irony of the importance of the 'I'

Goal: To understand we are all equal and our actions are based on what we perceive as positive intentions.

Duality: Without equipoise, we suspect we are the only ones with good intentions.

Epiphany: My ego shall not rule my opinions.

Affirmation: I trust myself to let go and be guided by my intuition.

The title 'The irony of the importance of the "I"' speaks volumes when we stop for a minute and observe the profound duality between how we talk to ourselves versus what we expect of others. There is often a large gap between the two. Beyond that, we are all different, so the power of interpretation allows us liberty and generosity in our impressions to genuinely communicate in an unbiased and honest manner. Misunderstanding is the landmine that surrounds every conversation, unless we present ourselves with an open mind, a clean heart and a silenced ego. Please be mindful that this refers not only to our conversations with others but includes the conversations we have with ourselves.

There is no measure of our own goodness save from our own polished eye. Without the polished eye, we tend to be our worst enemy and maker of our own misery, especially if we are functioning outward in. How shall we determine what we believe about ourselves? Should the constant ebb and flow of how life plays out determine who we are? Should we bow to the voices that reprimand or validate us as our mirror? We are our intimate companion from birth until we transition. Does this not beg that we must go within, be kind to ourselves and allow for a nurturing and comforting relationship with ourselves?

Responsibility, defined as the ability to respond appropriately, begs we begin with us. How do you speak to yourself? Are you silent within, simply observing through your intuition and keeping that as your ultimate guide? Or is your mind busy with your internal voice and events transpiring around you that keep you on your toes? Inviting an inner silence and a huge ice cream sundae of gratitude as our best friends and cheerleaders is truly the most blissful gift we can afford ourselves. What prevents it? We as human beings tend to practise huge caution in trusting the positive while it's so easy to denigrate ourselves. There is, of course, always the exception of the narcissists who can never question themselves nor their motives as the other extreme.

In its highest form, not judging is the equipoise and ultimate act of forgiveness. By recognising that mistakes and misunderstandings are a part of being human, not only do we become more empathetic, we also open ourselves to being more acutely aware. When we know that love and kindness towards ourselves and others is the only way forward, we stop being judgemental of ourselves, and, in turn, we become more understanding towards others. It is so obvious, yet how many of us actually practise these simple skills on a minute-by-minute basis, twenty-four hours a day, seven days a week and 365 days in a year?

Fostering curiosity rather than judgement leads to inner peace, self-acceptance, kindness and healthier relationships. Life is nuanced and requires a more broad-minded approach. Curiosity and non-judgement provide us a more balanced approach to life. Judgements are assumptions, not truths. They are about us being right in our own impressions and the other person being wrong because of our closed-mindedness and our egos. Imagine what we are feeding! They don't do any good or serve us in any way. Being curious is a kind and gentle approach that creates a detached and disarmed environment where it's clear that we are all different people, dealing with life as best we can. It breeds humility. Please watch yourself from a birds-eye view and discern and observe your own behaviour to silence the ego and engage from a stance of stillness.

When we take a moment to stop and sit still, we are able to listen to the whispers of our minds that can otherwise be lost in the fast-paced cacophony of our lives. By setting peace of mind as our highest standard, and organising our lives around it, we can let go of things that are weighing us down and shine bright, happy and fulfilled in being able to choose the best for ourselves without the pressure. We need to constantly remind ourselves that the pressure is self-imposed because of what society (and our egos) demand from us, rather than what we choose as our guideline with humility, discipline and integrity. We know that our quiet within breeds a more centred, compassionate and contented life.

There are no limitations on what we can be, do or have. We can make a masterpiece of our own lives. By changing the quality of our thinking, we can change the quality of our lives.

Use each day as an opportunity to improve, to be better, to get a little closer to our goals. The more we accomplish, the more we will be motivated to do and the higher we will reach. The harder we work for something, the greater we feel when we succeed. It begins simply with our own impressions of ourselves and cleaning the slate of unconscious slander or comparison that we garner towards ourselves or others.

We are our choices. Life presents us with a lot of decisions. They can be difficult and confusing, but we must persevere and choose what feels right to us, not what makes us look good to others. We cannot make progress without making sound decisions. We cannot make sound decisions without a quiet and humble mind. Sometimes the smallest decisions can change

IMPRESSIONISM - PERCEPTIONS AND ILLUSIONS

our lives forever, hence why our canvas requires us to first take care of our perceptions and illusions to clarify where we are with ourselves.

We complicate our lives so much. Our egos are responsible for giving us images of grandeur that are impossible to sustain, unless we are engaged in doing good for humanity. A balanced approach of humility, gratitude and witnessing beauty in every minute of every day is what creates an abundant inner being.

Challenge yourself with the following SRT – How Free Are You? – to observe yourself gently, and then review it again later.

Self-Reflective Tool 1.3: How Free Are You?,
www.gardenofayden.com/13howfreeareyou

ENTER THE GARDEN: MODULE 2
The Greenhouse – Self-Reflection

Purpose: We are learning to dismantle preconceived ideas and where they stem from. Our childhood and family experiences play a significant role in creating our understanding of the world and ourselves. We are contemplating our family maps to recognise what we perceive as truths. We ask ourselves if these truths remain valid today or are different from what we were labelled as. We question if our potential was limited. We delve into what we wish to free ourselves from and what we want to redefine.

Branch 2.1 – What were the contexts during my childhood?

Goal: To understand why my family was the way it was.

Duality: Cynical and quarrelsome vs. compassionate and loving.

Epiphany: My perception on my family has evolved.

Affirmation: I become humble to take a different eye on my impressions.

Rumi's wisdom says, 'The butterfly carries no memory of the caterpillar and that is why it is able to fly.'[2] In other words, a butterfly does not feel like a victim as it holds nothing from the past; it flies free. It is a beautiful metaphor to carry with us as we untangle our truths.

While keeping the butterfly in mind, here is another metaphor. Imagine there are many coloured threads all tangled together in knots. They represent us without all the awareness that we are capable of embodying. As we progress with untangling truths, imagine separating all the coloured threads and lining them up, each colour separated in its own line.

Before a client comes to see me, I request them to complete a thorough Garden of Ayden Discovery Form, in which there are many questions. It is a

---

2   Rumi, *Daylight: A daybook of spiritual guidance*, translated by Camille and Kabir Helminski (Shambhala Publications, 1990)

Word document, so it gives all the space to answer questions as deeply as necessary, allowing for full disclosure peacefully in full confidentiality. I study the Discovery Form prior to the client coming to see me. I will have fully absorbed the person by then, so we may immediately start resolving the issues deeply. It's an amazing process as I am able to map what I have read against the person's visual body language to deeply understand them. It's a magical process as I visibly witness shifts within the first session.

Far too often, our limiting beliefs are invisible, hidden within the layers of our subconscious minds. Our conscious minds will not necessarily bury layers easily. By outlining the detailed narrative of our lives within a precious document, there is a contextual map of patterns. It becomes like the epiphany that Ratatouille felt when he ate grapes with Camembert![3] It is rewarding, and we release the weight of the past effortlessly.

It was fascinating when I was hosting children's and parenting classes within a school. By working with both the parent and the child, I was able to quickly understand and bridge challenges discreetly. It felt so rewarding to be able to assist smoothly without having to raise the topics out loud. I simply worked at reframing the challenges peacefully and, at times, with humour. It worked beautifully.

---

3   B Bird and J Pinkava, *Ratatouille* (Pixar Animation Studios, 2007)

We are all capable of healing ourselves with this mirror of self-reflection. Taking a step back and being able to observe the events of our lives alongside the characters of our loved ones that impact us allows us to experience the epiphanies and thereafter quietly dissolve any chains.

Perhaps you are holding memories or pains that are not yours but inherited? If you've blamed yourself for different things that happened in your childhood, it is important to realise that it wasn't your fault. No one ever tells us that it's not our fault. There are things that happen in people's lives, but we believe we are responsible. What if you were to say to yourself now: it's not my fault? What happens? What changes in your world? How can you perceive yourself differently?

Letting go of these things is hard. I know, and I agree. It's not easy, but it's possible, and the only person who can do it is you.

In Part Three, I provide you with a link to *The Muse*, which will give you the opportunity to document all the precious self-realisations that occur during this journey. I suggest you wait until you reach that point before downloading it; continue with the SRTs for now, so that you may untangle everything piece by piece to achieve peace upon peace. I am smiling to myself imagining how many of you will be too curious to wait and will still download it now! Slow is fast and fast is slow. Why? Slow is fast when we do the work slowly and carefully to achieve the results we seek as soon as possible. Fast is slow because we precipitate and then presume the method doesn't work because we are in a hurry and rush through things. Please take your time and enjoy each moment and step of the process. I promise you it's joyful, and not as painful or difficult as you may imagine, irrespective of the heaviness of the past. You will feel gradually lighter and lighter as we progress.

Letting go may feel daunting but it's actually so much fun. You suddenly feel like you have magical powers because you are deciding to take control of what was always already yours: the power of choice. Everything is a choice, and we have the power to make any choice we wish. I wonder why we are not taught that at a young age.

A story from ten years ago that exemplifies this perfectly is the following. A client reached out after being recommended to come and see me. We had a brief call and then I sent him the Discovery Form to fill in depth. From what I read, I imagined an overweight man with a strong stutter. In walked a handsome, sparkling, suited suave gentleman who didn't stutter even once! He had chained himself within, truly believing and living his childhood map rather than releasing the past and celebrating who he had become.

We need to be vigilant to become aware of what we carry of ourselves within from our past that we must release. Since most people use their minds rather than their intuition, healing becomes more challenging, which is why we focus on awakening the intuition.

Please do the following Forgiveness Exercise, imagining yourself releasing and letting go of any wounds that you have been carrying and breathing a sigh of relief.

Self-Reflective Tool 2.1: Forgiveness Exercise, www.gardenofayden.com/21forgivenessexercise

Branch 2.2 – What impact does my childhood have on my today?

Goal: To reflect on what has created the way I am and how I react.

Duality: Self-accountable flow vs. victim dance.

Epiphany: I realise why I feel the way I feel and impact others.

Affirmation: I accept who I was then and who I am today.

Acknowledging and validating our childhood experiences enables us to not only rise beyond them with wisdom, it additionally allows us to develop a deeper empathy towards others. Maintaining them as a narrative through adult life will only hold us back. It is vital to honour our stories while releasing them to bring in a fresh wave of resilience and gratitude for all the lessons learnt. It allows for better self-preservation as well as energy to move forward with grace.

Something that helped me was to create a director in my mind. My director was and is sitting on a boat with a big gold medallion, a goatee and sunglasses. I always imagine the context of my life from the eye of my director. You may be amused; I urge you to try it. It has helped so many of my clients. It not only releases the drama; it brings in a great secondary sense with an acute feeling of freedom for the ability to shift our feelings at any moment. It helps me to watch myself and be aware of every reaction within or externally. It's almost as if I have my accountability partner at hand to constantly fine-tune my persona and my person. It also allows me to keep an eye on what is going on from a distance.

When you create a cognitive eye, it's like a bird's-eye view to watch and observe yourself, to monitor how you're behaving, and to see whether the appropriate behaviours are exactly as you would want them to be. You may observe things you are enacting that are not your best or your higher self. The cause is your unconscious triggers. By having this cognitive eye guiding you, you are able to monitor yourself.

We all have the ability to change anything that we wish to change about our lives by ourselves. Each of us has all the tools and resources within us, and please do not let anyone tell you the contrary. You want to become your own best friend. Sadly, those who actually practise this are few and far between, which I hope will now change. We are naturally not our own best friends. Our eye on ourselves is usually a difficult one.

Should you need motivation to discipline yourself to do this, let your loved ones be the scintilla that guides you. Your loved ones' sense of ease and effortless joy will be the result. It is not right that we should be responsible for causing any difficulty to those that surround us because of our little idiosyncrasies within ourselves. It is selfish to allow ourselves to remain unevolved or in a victim dance and allow those that surround us to bear the consequences. It's simply wrong. Had it never occurred before to consider this as a selfish act, may it now transform into an active agent of change, so that the people close to you, the ones you love, are able to see you as the gem that you are.

Just be you peacefully. Be your own best friend. Let go of all the resistance.

If you are tough on yourself, why? What's the cause of it? Is it necessary?

If you get angry about little things, what is the cause of it? Is it necessary?

Is it possible for you to reframe anything that comes across your path with a positive voice?

What does reframing mean? It's literally like changing the frame of a photograph. It's quite simple, and in the moment we are all able to do this. No one is prevented from changing anything they wish to within themselves, all that is required is a little awareness and the ability to grant ourselves permission. Everything is possible if you believe it is.

There are two ways of perceiving the word 'discipline'. There's discipline the noun and there's discipline the verb. Discipline the noun is structure; I have the discipline to always have a freshly baked chocolate cake at home. I have the discipline to keep fresh flowers. I have the discipline to be structured with my timings; I'm always on time. Discipline the verb is a negative connotation. For example, when you are running late, you start screaming at everyone else around you, which is not fair. If you've gone to sleep peacefully, had eight hours and woken up fresh, is your behaviour the same as if you've had a night with a crying baby, roadworks and a fight with somebody? The key is that your person has to stay intact, whatever happens, and that the boundaries we maintain with others are consistent.

I often use the word 'allow', as you will have noticed. The reason is that I don't believe I can impose myself upon you. I ask you to allow it because with your permission we can make these changes altogether and it's all possible.

Enjoy the contemplation in the SRT of asking yourself the reason why.

Self-Reflective Tool 2.2: The Reason Why Self-Assessment, www.gardenofayden. com/22thereasonwhyself-assessment

Branch 2.3 – By questioning my childhood beliefs, I see myself differently

Goal: To remove any false beliefs I may carry about myself.

Duality: Validate my truth vs. falsify to fit in.

Epiphany: Not everything I believed about myself is true.

Affirmation: I honour the child within me, while I change the perceptions I hold.

Change may seem difficult. Change may seem impossible, sometimes.

What does the word 'impossible' mean? 'I'm possible' people say, right? What are the things that have prevented us from being our highest and best? As a child, you get told you're unable to do something or you're not good at something and you decide to make it true. It requires questioning it again. It requires you to look in the mirror and say to yourself that what you were told does not have to be a truth. Who was judging you and based on what? Why is their opinion of you relevant to something subjective? There's no need to coin anything as fact. Everything is evolving at all times, as you are.

You can be anyone you want to be. You have to honour the child within you. We all have a child, an adult and a parent inside of us. If I'm having a conversation with my mother and it is my child that's awake and her parent, that conversation may be a little difficult. If my adult and her parent are awake, the conversation will be difficult. If it's her child and my parent, again it's not an easy conversation; however, if the adult within me is talking to the adult within her, we will laugh, joke and have fun together because we are not contextualising us, we are being wholesome grown-ups. I honestly believe that when each person practises this, we will dramatically reduce the quarrels in our world.

It is important to ask yourself this question during every conversation you have with different people. Are you being authentically yourself? Are you the same person, or are you wearing a mask? I know that I used to be ten different people, depending on who was sitting in front of me. I would behave differently because in my mind, that's what they would expect from me. As we get older, we may start questioning our truths and release any sense of peer pressure because you realise that your truths are more important than the views of others. You are able to synchronise your person, where your mind, heart, soul and body are fully aligned. Others may accept you gracefully when you accept yourself as you are.

Of course, the important part of that is about you accepting yourself. If there are things you are resisting, what are they and why? What is holding you back?

I had to do an improv class to be able to create the videos for these programmes because I struggled to sit in front of a camera. We all have our challenges. We all have our shyness or our difficulties in believing in ourselves or trusting that we are good enough. We can all be as good as we want to believe we are.

If your best friend sought your advice, how would you respond? Do you apply the same code of conduct and grace to yourself? Are you able to be kind to you? Looking after yourself allows you to look after other people. We criticise ourselves as victims because we have so much responsibility. It's actually not true. We can manage to look after ourselves peacefully with a quiet mind and belief in ourselves. This allows us to create any reality we want.

We are not victims of our circumstances, none of us. If your childhood was difficult, you can forgive it, and realise that it has carved the person you are, and can represent the strength formed deeply within you. Circumstances may not have been easy, however we are capable of moving beyond anything. We are able to become whoever we want to be, as long as we believe in ourselves. No one can do that for us; we can only do that for ourselves.

You may ask, how do we cultivate positive belief patterns? Start carving your best imagined journey and know that discipline breeds results. (Discipline the noun, not the verb.)

What challenges do you face every day while you ask yourself these questions? How do you look to overcome them? Are you complaining and repeating negative beliefs, or are you actually working towards wholesome thinking?

You know that if we keep repeating any negative projections we have, they stay within us. They don't actually help us to achieve anything. They almost say that if something negative happens, the more you're able to contain it, the sooner you can move past it.

Did you know that the subconscious mind does not know the difference between a past memory and something you are thinking now? If you start thinking about something that happened in the past and you relive it, you're causing your body to have the same reactions again. You don't want that for yourself. You want to be able to move forward positively.

Take a close look at the SRT, The Rules, and contemplate what you're allowing your mind to think about. Disciplining our minds like we discipline a muscle in our bodies allows us to actually change the future in a positive way. The key is to believe in you, and to believe that you are not a victim of your circumstance.

Self-Reflective Tool 2.3: The Rules,
www.gardenofayden.com/23therules

ENTER THE GARDEN: MODULE 3
The Season Of Your Heart – Self-Awareness And Self-Knowledge

Purpose: Having begun to self-reflect, we become more aware and able to define our ideas and thought processes. While re-evaluating our more deep-seated assumptions, we may acknowledge that we don't control anything around us. What we can control is ourselves. Self-change becomes the key to uncovering anything.

Branch 3.1 – Observing the pattern of my thoughts

Goal: To clearly understand the construct of my thoughts.

Duality: I cannot be full until I empty myself.

Epiphany: I am joining the dots of my misconceptions.

Affirmation: I will not judge myself nor harbour negative thoughts within me.

How are your levels of self-confidence, self-worth and self-esteem?

How do you feed yourself on a day that feels or looks gloomy?

How do you start your day? Do you decide that the world is against you if anything negative happens or do you actually perceive goodness in anything that's coming?

Friedrich Nietzsche uses the term *amor fati*,[4] a Latin phrase that translates to 'love of fate'. This concept encourages us to surrender and open ourselves to whatever happens in life – any dimension of anything that happens – while adopting the belief that everything that happens has a learning in it for us and finding meaning, even in the event of negative experiences. Sadly, even trauma becomes the birthplace of resilience, fortitude and wisdom.

From which eye do we coin our truths? Do we reflect upon our past and measure against it? Is it self-doubt that creeps in? How well do we know ourselves?

---

4   F Nietzsche, *The Joyous Science (Die fröhliche Wissenschaft)*, translated by Thomas Common (Friedrich Krug, 1910)

Are we reacting rather than responding to what's happening on a daily basis? How do we know?

Is it our mood that determines what happens? Is it mood that determines thoughts? Where do thoughts come from and where do they go? What is it that determines our communication?

We are fascinating creatures with so much more potential than we grant ourselves. We cannot but admire our inner make up. We cannot but marvel at the complexity of our beings. We must keenly observe how context affects our moods.

Create the context within to envision what you wish to create, picture it deeply within your imagination and witness it unfold.

It is true that we are a sum of all our experiences that result in our tacit knowledge. Defined and perceived accurately, every day we are accumulating further experience to achieve more. We use the difficult experiences as a springboard to propel us upwards and onwards. Let's compete with our past to make our future brighter.

If we walk into a meeting scared and nervous, that energy will transpire into the meeting. If we walk into a meeting confident, knowing that the outcome is going to be for the highest and best outcome and willing ourselves for it to be so, everything changes.

How do we determine what happens?

Are we willing to align to a beauty of something that we cannot see? Are we willing to actually play games with the universe and to say we are willing to take every chance to make this the best moment in every moment?

By doing that, we invite all sorts of positive outcomes. If we are doing something every day that scares us, at the end of the day we can celebrate just knowing we tried something that took us out of our comfort zone. The outcomes can change every day. Something that we perceive as negative today could be great tomorrow.

Will we ever know? Is negative self-doubt and questioning everything worth it? We're not controlling anything. To break the habit of negative thinking, ask yourself, what can I do today that will allow me to step forward?

If you bite your tongue every time you have a negative thought, what happens? You create a discipline. You discipline yourself to start thinking positively by catching yourself every time you entertain a negative thought. You discipline yourself bite by bite, to actually see positive in everything and everyone.

Other people's behaviour is a direct result of what and how we communicate. Hence, we are actually responsible for our positive communication. If you're busy thinking that somebody's treating you badly, smile at them. Apologise to them. Humble yourself in front of them. There's no reason why they should react badly with you.

If you are sensitive or sensitised, say, 'Well, this person is treating me badly.' Ask yourself if you've done something to create that situation or just observe them without any judgement and say, 'It's OK. I understand they're having a bad day and it will be better tomorrow.'

We cannot force people to be anything that we want them to be. What we can do is invite a positive reaction in the way we're behaving. If we walk down the street and somebody's frowning at us, if we smile at them they will immediately smile back. It's not possible that they don't, and in just the same light we make ourselves accountable for whatever happens. We don't control the weather. We can decide to love a cloudy day or a sunny day. Depending on where you live, it could be sunny or cloudy every day, so we tend to appreciate the opposite. It could be contrary to the norm, however that is our truth and we must be comfortable with it.

We must enjoy every moment of every day for what it is. Negating ourselves negates our impact, negates our communication, negates the results. Adopt the discipline of self-correction. It's magical. Test it. See what happens.

Ask yourself: am I accountable or am I making other people accountable for my behaviour?

Lastly, once again, are we victims? Are you behaving like a victim? Or are you saying, 'I'm accountable, I'm responsible and it's all going to be fine'?

The reason this untangling is kept in the simplest form possible is to be able to untangle ourselves easily, step by step. Rest assured that as we progress, it becomes even lighter and lighter. Please be honest with yourself when you fill in the next SRT, Impact of My Behaviour on Others – it's a worthy truth fest.

Self-Reflective Tool 3.1: Impact of My Behaviour on Others, www.gardenofayden.com/31impactofmybehaviouronothers

Branch 3.2 – A close look in the mirror

Goal: To see the knots I imposed upon myself that require untangling.

Duality: Any negative I perceive in others are seeds that are fermented within me.

Epiphany: I accept myself with all my strengths and subtleties.

Affirmation: To free myself from self-imposed limitations, I no longer allow any negative thoughts to influence me.

Let's re-evaluate. What happens if I leave people free without my judgement and I just simply observe?

What happens is there's oxygen in every situation.

Imagine you and the person in question are both holding a rope. They tug and you tug, and it just goes on relentlessly and endlessly, creating a pointless rollercoaster of emotions. When you visualise putting down the rope metaphorically – gently, of course, so that the other person doesn't fall – the person suddenly loses power over you and is no longer able to tug at your heartstrings anymore. There's no energetic connection between you because you have unattached yourself from the situation. It's a fantastic tool towards self-preservation and releases any impressions from the past. You will feel a strong sense of relief. It may make you initially tired, since you are letting go of a heavy burden that you have been perhaps carrying for a long time. You are releasing yourself from their grip and can thereafter see the person from a distance without allowing them to affect you in any way. You can actually breathe into the moment.

What happens is there's no expectation so there's no push and pull. There's no one expecting anything and therefore a real conversation can be had. How much of the time do we spend waiting for someone to do something we want, as opposed to letting them do what they want?

What happens is I stop thinking about me. I stop thinking about my desires, my take, what I need, and I start just embracing the moment. I am just there, observing. Nothing going on, just breathing peacefully. When I let go of the moment, suddenly everything changes dimension. How?

Test it. See what happens. The minute we are not attached to a situation or an outcome, our whole environment turns. It completely changes. Even our reactions evolve, our facial expressions lighten. The glint in our eye changes. Our cheekbones are more relaxed, absolutely everything changes.

A person will receive you differently if you're relaxed than if you seem uptight and waiting for something. All these things are felt and noticed in the split of a second. Even within a couple or between a parent and child, the minute tension is diffused, everything can evolve. So much of the time we wait for someone to do something we want. We nag, we give the cold treatment or we're passive-aggressive and there's just no purpose to it all. Let it go. Letting it go is the best thing one can do. We do not actually control anything.

Imagine I'm fifteen years old and you are three years old and I want you to learn algebra. How are you to learn algebra at three years old? Who is foolish in this situation, me or you? I am being silly because I am insisting, and I am getting angry that you're not understanding algebra. We're at different stations of life. We don't necessarily understand each other perfectly. How can I expect you to know everything I know, and how can I expect you to deem what I know as important versus what you know? As human beings, metaphorically we are all at different stations in our journey, and we all have our individual experiences of life, indoctrination and character. Why would we presume someone to understand us perfectly? Why is it that we take anything that is different to our perspective as being wrong? Why do we believe that our views are the only correct way to perceive things?

Creating boundaries, allowing respect for people to be who they want to be and giving ourselves the freedom to be who we are, while treading carefully, shifts any interaction. Listen with awareness. Re-establish our norms based upon principles of respect.

Letting go invites magic. We become masters of discernment. We can discern situations because we are quiet inside of ourselves. We are able to look at situations from a distance without actually making it about us.

You remove the *you* from the equation and you suddenly observe things that you have never noticed before because your mind is quiet. You start seeing signs and signals everywhere. You think about someone, and they call. That's the value and beauty when synchronicity awakens within us.

The minute we quieten our minds and allow the realm of simply being, we invite so much mystery into our lives. We can see things that we have never seen before. The flowers smell more fragrant. The sea looks more intense. The sky looks more stunning. Everything changes. Finding that quiet, instead of always thinking about you, allows you to open a dimension of life that's beautiful. Will you try it?

Let's take distance and be more sympathetic in our gaze upon people. Let's be sympathetic and actually alter our perspective of what we are looking at. As we've talked about the pink glasses, let's change glasses and see things from a different eye.

When you begin to practise this, you will marvel at how it works beautifully in stretching yourself. It's developing this flexible strength where you're willing to allow the oxygen in and breathe to a distinctive dimension of being. Does it sound crazy? Try it. It works.

Branch 3.2's SRT is a lot of self-discovery as I invite you to complete the three personality tests within it. If you do not already know them, you will thoroughly enjoy deepening the enquiry into your nature, which will add so much more depth into this continued journey. Enjoy!

Self-Reflective Tool 3.2: Personality Tests,
www.gardenofayden.com/
32personalitytests

Branch 3.3 – The renovation of my thoughts

Goal: To believe I can change the outcome of any situation with the power of my thoughts.

Duality: I relinquish the illusions of grandeur to genuine growth.

Epiphany: I feel at peace. I didn't know I wasn't until I was.

Affirmation: I trust myself and know I am able to succeed at whatever I put my heart and mind to.

Who or what are we using as a measure of the meaning of success? Is it an inner or an outer state?

Success is a measure of how you feel inside. It is linked to you with you. It's got nothing to do with what anyone else thinks of you. It's about how you perceive yourself.

If we're busy wanting to look good for other people and successfully doing so while beating ourselves up on the inside, that's not doing a great job. When success is linked to how we feel, it allows us to be anything we want to be. It empowers us to the maximum and in turn creates the results we seek. It involves the measure of how we feel about ourselves after a long day. Being honest with ourselves about what motivates us. Whatever our truth is, there is no reason to judge ourselves by it. We accept where we are in our journey, and if we are not happy with it we make the decision to make a roadmap of changes we seek. We create the desire to constantly work on being the best version of ourselves. Nothing remains stagnant. All the power is within us.

Let's now go into some topics that we often find difficult. What is the notion of trust? How do you know if you can trust someone? How do you measure if you can trust them? Is it based upon them or you?

Please allow me to suggest something. I know I can trust someone or a situation because I trust myself. If someone lets me down, I say to myself, 'Oops, my mistake. I trusted them so it was my mistake because it was my misjudgement.' If my intuition is polished well enough, I will have all the elements to unlock my best guide. Perhaps I was following my mind or a romantic notion rather than my intuition?

I don't hold on to it and say, 'How dare they do that to me,' because it was me that trusted them in the first place. It was me that allowed it. Nobody signs a contract to say that you can trust them. If it does happen, you are lucky, because we never can know unless we are focused within.

The notion of trust has to be a notion of trusting ourselves. It increases our accountability and doesn't allow us to be swept away without a second thought. Let's look at love. If I love someone, where is the love? The love is inside me. How the other person loves me is their problem. It's not about me. It's about their feelings inside of them.

If I love you and I buy you a gift, I'm doing it because it makes me happy that my heart is full of love for you. How is it possible that I should wait for the other person to respond in exactly the way I want them to? It doesn't make sense somehow. If I am loving, then I give because it makes me joyful, not because I am waiting for something in return.

The whole value of love, trust and respect all begins with you. Your world will change completely if you adopt these principles. The more you love someone and give them the best of you without any expectation, the more you feel expansive and blessed. If they do something nice for you, you are so surprised because you are not expecting anything; you're just happy loving them. You may think that this makes you vulnerable – this is your ego awakening.

If the other person doesn't love you the way you want them to, is it because they are bad? Is it because they are selfish? Is it because they are mean? It cannot be. It is a measure of your character that you are projecting. They are their own person. They have their own character. They have their ups and downs. They were nurtured differently than you were in their childhood. Their understanding of love is different to yours. You've chosen to love someone; accept them for who they are. Sounds simple, right? I know it's not easy sometimes, because we get so confused with reactions people have.

If you allow it to be that you're in control of you, the only person whose accountability you need to pay attention to is yours, and you're giving your highest and best. You will only receive the highest and best if the person is good for you. If not, you will understand sooner rather than later. It's when we overstep our boundaries, demand and expect too much, that the other person becomes resistant and chooses to respond differently. Thereafter we react negatively, and it all goes haywire. There's no need. There's no use of it. It accomplishes nothing.

Be unattached in your stance, aspiring for the highest and best. Give your best. A lot of times, people bribe. They say, 'If he's not going to do that for me, I'm not going to do that for him.' It doesn't work like that. Give, be kind, be generous, be trusting because you trust yourself, and see what happens. Follow your intuition and allow it to guide you.

It is you that chooses how you feel. You are the architect in defining what you want to feel. Your duty is to feel responsible for being authentically you, and happy to be you. Ask yourself if you're making any demands or having expectations of people or things that are a little unreasonable.

We're not questioning other people here; we are questioning ourselves. We will be looking into relationships deeply when we reach Looking At The I With A Deeper Eye in Part Three.

Let's polish our mirrors, question the value of our thoughts and ask ourselves the right questions to enlighten ourselves first. Align the thoughts that go through our minds peacefully so that we can step forward, onwards and upwards, gracefully every day, feeling happy, feeling peaceful and constantly growing.

In the SRT, Self-Reflective Journey, we look within to establish where we are with ourselves and give ourselves the roadmap of where we wish to evolve further.

Self-Reflective Tool 3.3: The Journey,
www.gardenofayden.com/
33thejourney

ENTER THE GARDEN: MODULE 4

Mother Nature Vs. Mother Nurture – Self-Accountability

Purpose: *Becoming more aware of the past patterns of the limitations of our ideas and thought processes, we quickly realise that we are self-accountable. We have the power to choose our thoughts. We analyse what behaviours we would like to improve upon. We discard preconceived notions of others or even ourselves, and we celebrate our strengths. We embrace our mistakes with relief and enjoy who we are. We'll learn to be comfortable with what we don't know and happily strive to learn more.*

Branch 4.1 – The correlation of heart, mind, body and soul

Goal: To align myself completely with all aspects of my being.

Duality: The inner critic is transformed to be my highest taskmaster.

Epiphany: When I align my heart, body, soul and mind, my intuition awakens.

Affirmation: I surrender and listen to my intuition.

Have you been watching and observing your thought patterns? Have you started releasing your inner critic or are you still holding on to it for dear life?

Here are some tools to assist you in a process of releasing things consciously.

Your bubble of light

Every time you think a negative thought, it's a great idea to bite your tongue to start releasing any inner negative critic. You become immediately cognisant of the negative patterns that appear to reframe them in that instant.

To contain your energy and hold on to everything positive that's in your world while maintaining your boundaries, imagine that you are surrounded by armour of a glowing bubble of light. It can be a green bubble, it can be a golden bubble, it can be any colour you wish. You're in this bubble at all times and the bubble is a protection that surrounds you. Any energy that approaches you is touching the outer, glowing light of the bubble, unable to pierce through. Between the edge of the bubble and your heart, everything is completely peaceful, irrespective of your surroundings. You are constantly safeguarded against any impact of anything negative coming towards you, as your energy is secure and contained by your protective shield.

Zipping up your energy

In the morning, before you head out of the door, a good thing to do is lock up your energy. To zip up your energy, literally take your hand from the base of you to over your head, mimicking the movement as if you are doing up a zip. This allows you to function well within yourself, enables you to contain your energy without it dispersing too much and, of course, it shields you.

Imagining your fingers and toes as air valves

I'd like you to imagine that your fingers and toes are air valves. Close your eyes and embed the image of your fingers and toes as large air tubes as you take a deep breath in and a deep breath out. Your fingers and toes from here on act as air valves, not allowing any negative energy to be stored within you. Anything negative that comes to you – be it a thought, a word, a tone of voice – goes in and releases itself through your fingers or toes, or both. This way, there's no tension that can actually sit within your body at any given time. It's a wonderful healing and self-preservation exercise.

Stop technique

I have embedded the 'stop technique' so deeply within me that as I write these words I am already beginning to yawn! The minute I think the word 'stop', I start to yawn, and this will happen to you too as you develop this practice.

The first thing you do is say 'stop'. You close your eyes, take three deep breaths, and as you become regular in this practice, your body may start to tingle as you release any unwanted, tired or stagnant energy. Get in the habit of doing this regularly, and practise it between meetings when you are back to back. You may leave one meeting and once you get in the car, you say, 'stop', you take a deep breath and you will end up yawning all the way to your next meeting. You will arrive completely fresh, alert and aware. You will feel as if the previous meeting has never happened. This is another great self-preservation tool to help you release your inner critic, which even allows your best ideas to emerge while you are yawning.

Monitoring the impact of your mind on your body

Why is it assisting you to release your inner critic? It's because any impact in the mind affects the body. If we are able to monitor ourselves consciously to know that we have to say 'stop' and we have to recentre and rebalance ourselves, then everything flows easier and we cope much better.

Say 'stop'. Take a deep breath and release.

Keeping salt on you

I would like you to place a dollop of table salt inside a tissue. Fold up the tissue carefully. Gentlemen, kindly place it in your pocket every morning before beginning your day. Ladies, place it in the centre of your bra so that it is unnoticeable. This is another method of caring for your energy, and its impact is astonishing. You feel less drained and maintain good energy throughout your day without absorbing any negative energy.

As you know, the mind is a theatre of imagination and what we're doing is awakening our intuition because our gut feeling is actually the strongest part of us. By disciplining ourselves in keeping our energy flowing responsibly in our bodies, we can slowly silence the inner mind, which is the inner critic. We may start awakening the gut feeling – also known as the intuition – that guides us peacefully to positive outcomes.

Breathing and exercising with awareness

Discipline – the noun, of course – the discipline of daily exercise. If we resist going to the gym, practising yoga, doing something, it works against us. What if you were to say to yourself, 'I am exercising daily, even if I'm just walking to the car, and I'm breathing consciously'. It's quite simple, right? You are just breathing in and out. Inhaling and exhaling and allowing yourself to humbly walk with awareness. Breathe with awareness. Start taking baby steps towards fulfilling everything you want, not by aggressing yourself. Do this by being kind to yourself, saying, 'I can do this. I want to do this. I'm happy to do this and I am thoroughly enjoying the process.'

The following SRT, Practice Makes Perfect, assists you by giving you something to record your progress as you engage with these practices. As it says, practice truly does make perfect.

Self-Reflective Tool 4.1: Practice Makes Perfect, www.gardenofayden.com/ 41practicemakesperfect

Branch 4.2 – A deep breath of forgiveness while releasing triggers

Goal: To realise what was creating my reactions.

Duality: Silencing the dualities within brings peaceful understanding of the external dualities.

Epiphany: I can remove violence and aggression as useless tools in my daily journey.

Affirmation: My person becomes free of any triggers as my negative impressions are altered and released.

We all know a story similar to the banker who becomes a drummer after he goes through burnout. Was it his original calling to be a drummer or was being a banker in the corporate world unfulfilling? Did he burn out because of the pressure of an unbalanced life? Did he feel out of place, constantly triggered in a competitive heartless environment of dog eat dog? There are endless possibilities to every scenario that happens to many. Let's work on prevention rather than cure.

Do you overdramatise situations? Do you let your mind toy with terrible outcomes, getting flustered easily, predicting the future negatively? How do you know that events will have negative outcomes unless you are projecting them, thereby inviting them?

What we project is an invitation. I beg you, silence the narrative within and begin trusting the silence. It's time to live it and project positively. The sky is the limit. We leave ourselves open. Everything depends on you.

After doing the Personality Tests in SRT 3.2, if we had not already considered the diversity that exists, our perspectives widen to realise how many different possibilities there are to define characters, with absolutely no right or wrong. When we are getting triggered by others due to misunderstanding, or when we perceive malintent, we stop in our tracks to reconsider. How much of the disharmony in our world is due to not only different natures of people but also the complexity of people profiling, indoctrination and professional acumen (or lack thereof)? Perhaps we don't yet fully realise that embracing differences is the beginning of harmony.

Let's start with the simple questions that query our inner voices:

- Whose life are we living?
- What narrative have we built to justify and reinforce it?
- Is it our ultimate truth or have we conditioned ourselves to believe it?
- Are we sure it's ours or are we programmed to live up to expectations?

I'm not suggesting you rebel against anything; I'm simply suggesting you prevent any cognitive dissonance and fight contrary voices within. I once asked a young client to explain cognitive dissonance and he brilliantly replied, 'I love to swim but I hate the water.' It's possible to love the water and hate to swim, but how do you hate the water and love to swim? When we are battling two opposite views within us we create inner conflict and turmoil.

The question begs: are you silently rebelling within?

Having experienced all the releasing exercises in 4.1, you realise how easy it is to release the tension that your body holds, to find a state of naturalness in the flow of your body. I sincerely hope you continue working on this SRT to monitor your progress.

Once mastered, these tools change the quality of our everyday lives. We can all acknowledge that when something is misaligned in the mind, it creates tension in the body. Once this truth sinks in deeply, we realise how vital it is to not only keep a healthy body, a healthy mind must accompany it.

When our bodies react, do we usually immediately appreciate what it's telling us? Can we understand it or are we perplexed? If we have our minds, hearts, bodies and souls aligned, our bodies gives us clues as blessings. The ability to live with a receptive open heart, mind and body is the art that is the perfect home for our intuition. We remain grateful to the signs that the universe offers us. (It is the cynical ones who may react to this and say it's romantic rubbish, and then sadly awaken during the burnout as described of the banker-turned-drummer in the beginning of this branch – let's help them prevent that!)

Let's begin identifying the triggers that we house. Releasing the triggers and the negative energy holding us back is a crucial step in this journey. As we become more aware and intuitive, we identify things and let them go so much faster, when we are observing from a bird's-eye view.

We are able to identify people stealing our energy, those negating us or who may be toxic for us. No judgement; this is purely based on you with you. Identifying people you feel are more like drains than fountains in your world. You may have already, or you will begin to feel this easily as you become deeply connected to quickly distinguish the fountains from the drains. Ensure that you take a break, take distance. Most importantly, ensure that you're giving the best of yourself to those you love.

It's time to disarm any triggers.

We forgive ourselves, forgive others. Plant the seeds of our intentions to do the best we can and release any remaining triggers peacefully. Push yourself. Test the limits to open your mind as vastly as you feel able to now.

When you open the QR code below, you will have a list of seventy-five triggers to contemplate. The way I like to use this document with clients is to get them to identify a name, a specific feeling or situation that they scribble next to the trigger to isolate, identify and permanently disarm the trigger. The beauty is that once the trigger is narrowed out, it will effortlessly vanish. Remember to use your director's view to assist you with some humour. A client had his boss dressed in clown outfits. It was fascinating how smoothly and seamlessly all his work triggers vanished.

I invite you to develop your director while you work on all the triggers.

Self-Reflective Tool 4.2: Triggers,
www.gardenofayden.com/
42triggers

Branch 4.3 – Looking at my definition of harmony

Goal: To consider my values and whether I am practising them consistently.

Duality: The battles worth fighting for illuminate my values.

Epiphany: My actions are no longer a result of outside influences as I put down the rope and live according to my own values.

Affirmation: By living my values on a daily basis, I will attract the same values that exist in each human being.

We are all self-accountable.

We know that we attract what we are. If we're attracting bad or difficult experiences, we need to ask ourselves if we invite them. We choose our battles carefully, and examine the values that we uphold, to know what to release. When we have defined and are enacting our values on a daily basis, nothing stands in our way.

For example, I prioritise my work for humanity, my son, my partner and my parents. I am aware of the limitations of time. Time is precious, waste it wisely. How do you prioritise your time?

When we balance our checkboxes on a daily basis – something for the mind, workwise; something for the heart, love wise; something for the spirit, emotionally or spiritually; and, last but definitely not least, something physical. When we consciously practise balance on a daily basis, we find an agreeable balance in our lives.

The SRT for 4.3 is a document called Battles Worth Fighting For. This is in itself a roadmap to walk through any questions, where the answer will present itself. It will assist in putting out fires as well as ensuring prevention of any. It also provides validation with the internal rewards we seek, that may silently stimulate our daily lives.

Values are anything we want them to be. Being certain we are inviting and enacting the values we believe in converts suffering into gold, magically. With these little changes – removing negative habits, replacing them consciously – the fear disarms itself and courage arises.

When we want something, we have to first give it. When we want love, we give love. When we want to receive compassion, we give compassion. We cannot be entitled to expect to receive things unless we're actually giving them ourselves.

From which eye do we choose to perceive the world around us? If we focus on natural beauty and the joy of what is, we fill ourselves with constant bliss. This feels obvious, yet we need to ensure we are constantly practising it. The more thankful we are for the love we receive and the beauty we perceive, the more we will be filled with abundance and a magical flow.

Harmony is a big word. Being harmonious is a lovely state of being. We may all enact it. It requires self-accountability and discipline (the noun) with regular practice. Be proud and passionate about the things you love and believe in, the people you care about, and the causes that you hold close to your heart. When you give your all to something, it creates so much energy that even a little bit of commitment and hard work goes a long way.

We all have our own unique strengths and weaknesses. Let's take ownership of our experiences and memories that have carved the person we are. Let's celebrate them, knowing we have the resilience to face whatever comes. We continue to cultivate and refine ourselves by growing and expanding our understanding of ourselves, thereby understanding the world around us and where we stand in it.

What are you going to practise today? Who do you trust? Know that trust has to start with *you* – you trusting yourself allows you to trust other people. Deepening self-trust resolves the issue of trusting others.

Who do you respect and admire? Do you respect and admire yourself? What is it that you respect and admire about yourself that other people can respect and admire too?

It is not easy to see the positive outcomes of our actions in the beginning, but with persistence and perseverance, we can develop ourselves and accomplish anything we put our minds to.

Remember, this is a mirror. Everything's about you and the questions you ask yourself. If integrity is your value, are you practising integrity with everybody you meet and everything you do? If honour is your value, are you acting honourably?

My own positive self-worth remains intact, regardless of external noise. Let this be the mantra we repeat to ourselves to maintain our inner strength, regardless of the inconveniences. It's the best way to maintain our inner certitude during uncertain times. We must continue to trust ourselves and our capacity.

All of the values can be and are yours – they're all resources within you in any case. What is your highest and best, and how are you going to do it?

This is a harmonious journey; please take your time to absorb and enjoy it, and take a look at the next SRT to deeply contemplate the battles worth fighting for.

Self-Reflective Tool 4.3: Battles Worth Fighting For, www.gardenofayden.com/43battlesworthfightingfor

ENTER THE GARDEN: MODULE 5

Waltzing In The Wilderness Or In Wisdom – Responsibility

Purpose: Becoming self-accountable prepares the way to accepting that we own the responsibility – the ability to respond appropriately – in our interactions with others in a judgement-free way. How people respond to us depends on how we communicate. We improve any communication if we focus on the role we play, and this freedom allows us to improve our relationships and interact more peacefully with anyone.

Branch 5.1 – The importance of graceful communication

Goal: To learn how my internal dialogue impacts myself and others.

Duality: Let go of the repetitive narrative to contain peace.

Epiphany: All reactions are based on how I myself communicate.

Affirmation: When I leave no other choice than elegance, it will reign.

What does the word responsibility mean to you?

We all have moments where we think, 'I have so much responsibility and there's so much burden to carry!' The word 'responsibility' actually means the ability to respond appropriately. This must come as a relief because it truly lightens the load. When responsibility is defined as my ability to speak correctly in every moment, it increases my sense of accountability and reduces this undefinable weight that many of us carry around with us unconsciously. We each have a responsibility to communicate our thoughts meticulously and use our words carefully in every moment.

Have you managed to dislodge the internal chatter? Is it gone yet? Are you still thinking about how other people are reacting to you? Haven't you started looking at life from behind their eyes yet? By looking at life from behind the eyes of others, you're no longer holding on to any sensitivity, and you are focused on the other person with a quiet mind. In desiring a positive outcome in your communication with the other person, you are now handling with care to ensure that you have the best results. You are no longer walking on eggshells.

Often, what happens when we're not aware of this is that we tend to say whatever's on our minds because we're upset, we're angry and we want the other person to understand what we're thinking.

If we concentrate on where the other person is coming from, it doesn't mean that we don't say the things we want to say, it's just that we speak more assertively and kindly. We can still transfer the same message to them. We're not attacking without consideration of where they are. Watching somebody allows you so much more freedom because you're looking at them and understanding them. You care about how they feel, even if you're upset, and you're monitoring your own reactions. Your intention is to have a positive outcome.

If I speak congruently, I can get a better result. Congruence doesn't mean that you're placating somebody, as you will see. Yet, you are consenting to speak peacefully for the same outcome. Anger makes our heads red. It doesn't allow us to speak with truth. We say things we don't mean, which we later regret. It's a waste of good energy. You may think it makes you feel good in the moment, thanks to your ego, but once the moment has passed, it becomes much more complex to find resolution. Why do that to yourself?

What if we make it a rule that from here on, you are going to say what you mean and mean what you say? Already, if you are not angry or if you're saying things out of anger, this cancels it out.

Say what you mean and mean what you say forces you to speak peacefully with premeditated thought to make sure you don't want to hurt the other person and that you want to get positive results for you both. Again, it's not about being right.

What we need to do is get comfortable with the discomfort, even if we know the other person has done something wrong (or what we perceive as wrong). They may not perceive it as wrong, and we need to get our heads around that.

You look for a way to make it OK, or you find a way to allow you both to find reason without too much noise. By just having the ability to perhaps show the other person your mirror and get them to imagine themselves in your shoes. If you say, 'I'd like you to imagine the example that if I was in your shoes and I spoke to you like this, would you like it?' They will say 'no', and you'll say, 'Well, please consider how you speak to me.' It can be handled congruently, peacefully and with grace, where you may develop beautiful communication, which improves every day in every way. May all our conversations be graceful.

Do you feel responsible for the way a conversation plays out or are you still busy blaming somebody else? When we blame, we're pushing the responsibility off us and making another person responsible. For how long can we do that? What if we choose that elegance is the only way forward, that we want to have a nice dynamic? You want someone to remember you as being sympathetic, empathetic, kind, cheerful and resilient. Everything is possible. How are you going to practise it?

The SRT for 5.1 is about styles of communication. It distinguishes the differences between being assertive, passive, aggressive and passive-aggressive in different situations. It's amazing to understand the way we communicate and to decipher how those around us communicate. Read through it once, and then go through it again, imagining the people closest to you to discern the style of each. It may even be that, depending on the scenario, you switch between them. Let's untangle our communication styles with the persistence for all of us to become assertive and let go of the rest.

Self-Reflective Tool 5.1: Communication Style, www.gardenofayden.com/51communicationstyle

Branch 5.2 – The kaleidoscope of non-verbal communication

Goal: To be introduced to tools to evaluate how I dance together with others.

Duality: Letting go of the fight for familiarity to embrace the unfamiliar.

Epiphany: I no longer judge anyone based on their behaviour but will believe there is good intention motivating it.

Affirmation: By improving my non-verbal skills, everyone around me changes their behaviour positively.

It takes seventeen muscles to smile and forty-nine muscles to frown.

This work is about practical compassion. From my experience with this type of work since 2012, focusing on practical compassion brings the highest results. Simple, straightforward and to the point. This, of course, doesn't suit those who dislike that I do not humour the ego. I look to immediately shed it for the person to be free to live to their highest and best.

I have understood the expression, 'The road to hell is paved with good intentions.'[5] There are complicated people in our world who are simply not interested in their divine power. They wish to lament and listen

---

5   St Francis de Sales, *Correspondence: Lettres d'Amitié Spirituelle* (written 1640; printed by Desclée De Brouwer, 1980)

to themselves speak. There is no interest in genuine healing. May each type of person awaken to their divine calling.

Body language speaks volumes. When we walk into a room, our body language precedes us. People get an immediate impression about us; we don't get two chances to make a first impression. This is so important in our world of today with so much social media. Are we displaying ourselves as we wish to be understood?

When sitting with our arms folded, unconsciously most people will consider us to be a little closed, cut off and distant, while this is probably the furthest thing from our minds. We do not realise the impression we are giving off.

When we sit somewhere with arms open and someone says something that sensitises us and makes us feel uncomfortable, we will immediately fold our arms. Why? Because we want to protect ourselves. We psychologically think that we feel protected if we close ourselves.

Is it worth closing ourselves? No, because what you want to do is be open to communicate and willing to embrace another person's ideas and thoughts. If a schoolteacher is standing with their arms closed, they look stern and strict to the children in front of them.

THE HUMAN TOUCH

When you walk into a room smiling, with your eyes wide open and maybe with your hands behind your back, it shows an easy disposition and a willingness to engage. This is such an important aspect of our well-being because we may sometimes wonder how people are responding to us, while we're not considering how we're actually approaching them.

If you're shy and you don't want to look someone in the eyes, and your habit is always looking down, there is an important trick to learn. Look at the person in between their eyebrows. They cannot notice that you are looking at them in between the eyes – they think you are looking at them in the eyes – while it gives you the comfort to know that you may maintain your stature. This is a great exercise for children to learn and it immediately dispels their shyness. Children don't like to be called shy, and it happens all too often that parents disregard this. More on all these topics in the upcoming books!

Let's say you walk into the room, and you notice someone sitting in front of you and glaring at you from head to toe, observing every detail of what you are wearing and how you look. How does that feel? It's extremely uncomfortable for anyone to be exposed to this, hence it is important to refrain. Many people do this without even realising that they are doing it. It is most definitely not a nice thing, and this behaviour sadly speaks volumes about a person.

Having respect while engaging with someone is expressed by looking at them in the eyes briefly with a smile, a nod or an acknowledgement of some type. This is a sign of respect. It is nice when a gentlemen stands up from the table when a lady approaches or everybody stands up when somebody elderly approaches. These dignified signs of respect, which are perhaps considered old-school culture, are lovely gestures. Chivalry is important to breed the correct values within and around us all. When we are considering other people's feelings, we are paying attention to what we can do to make them happy, especially at home among our families.

When you are sitting on a bus and an old lady gets on, do you stand up and offer your place with a smile? There are additional blessings that come to you from other people – strangers – if you are aware and paying attention.

Little gestures towards strangers go a long way and make you feel happy. If you are doing something nice for a stranger, it makes you smile. Children, in one of our classes, would hand out roses to absolute strangers. It helped them get over any barriers of shyness they may have, and they would feel so gratified by the beautiful smile they would receive in return from the stranger. Of course, the stranger is also delighted by this act of kindness. I hope every teacher across the world will practise this.

How many little acts of kindness can you do and thereafter witness how much you will cherish the results? It's a magical feeling that I cannot recommend enough. Acts of kindness for others bring you happiness.

Generosity does not have to be a monetary gesture. Being generous with others – even with a sense of humour, breaking the ice, letting people feel comfortable in your presence, making fun of yourself and not giving yourself too much importance – all these things work wonderfully well in making others feel comfortable, peaceful and happy.

The next SRT is about fine-tuning our behaviour and measuring action vs. intention. It's about determining your bird's-eye view against your inner intent.

Self-Reflective Tool 5.2: Action Vs Intention,
www.gardenofayden.com/
52actionvsintention

Branch 5.3 – The kaleidoscope of verbal communication

Goal: To see that everyone has different ways of communicating, and to become assertive in managing it.

Duality: Timid or self-righteous vs. lover of truth more than pretence.

Epiphany: I am mastering the art of diplomacy and peaceful interactions.

Affirmation: I will not judge others and will only interact with the highest good of each person that I may encounter.

What does the word tact mean to you?

Just as non-verbal communication is so important, the words you use reflect upon you. We have already established that anything anyone says speaks about *them*, not the other person.

I provided you with the SRT of Communication Styles in 5.1, and hope you will have had a chance to read through it and ascertain your feelings about your communication skills and those that surround you. Below, I wish to explain further so that all this may be absorbed deeply to create the real shifts you wish to see.

How do we respond to different types of behaviour?

People who are aggressive – those who feel the need to be right all the time or little bullies that our children face in school – insist on wanting to be right. They will walk in, sit down, belittle you and make you feel bad. They'll do what it takes to make themselves look bigger, taller, stronger and right. How do you respond to it?

We feel sorry for them and take nothing personally. Someone who's being a bully must have been aggressed or bullied and has no peace or calm within. We handle aggression quietly and respectfully. We don't put ourselves down, and we allow them to start reflecting upon how they're behaving. We don't judge them. We look from behind their eyes and wonder.

I'm not suggesting you accept this type of behaviour. If your ego stands up to them, sadly, at times, their response becomes more enraged and prevents the self-reflection and ability to change. It is best to work on disarming the aggression with empathy, rather than fuelling it.

Passive people will look meek, like they want to fail. They'll want you to rescue them. What do you do with that?

We may feel sorry for them, but placating them is not going to help them in the long run; feeling sorry for them only results in them feeling worse. We give energy and offer inspiration.

Feeling sorry for ourselves is perpetuating misery by regurgitating and repeating the same issues over and over. It is sadly not possible to improve a situation unless we lift ourselves up. Asking for help vulnerably allows us to be responded to positively. If we are nagging or forcing, we do not encourage desire in others to assist.

Passive-aggressive people will confuse you. They pretend they're being nice, but you will leave with this icky, eerie feeling of not understanding what's going on. Being passive, aggressive or passive-aggressive to manipulate someone has zero use. It is not a useful strategy.

Assertive people say what they mean and mean what they say. They speak clearly, congruently, happily and joyfully. Being assertive is allowing vulnerability and speaking truths in a measured way, even while upset or angry.

The behaviour we enact is worth considering. We tend to judge other people based upon our own mindsets. With good intentions, people's behaviour can often be shocking. We remain comfortable with discomfort, breathe deeply, continue to practise our integrity and observe carefully how other people are flowing and functioning. We refrain from attacking them, blaming them or being suspicious that they have bad intentions; it's not helpful.

It's worth listening to our intuition because it has the answers, and our verbal communication must stay aligned to who we are with our integrity and all our values intact.

I will quieten my mind to connect with my deeper self and understand the subtle voices of my intuition.

Empathy allows us to look deeply at the 'why'. Imagine a child tells you that they don't feel like their father trusts them. You question why. They say, 'Because when he asks me if I've done my homework and I say "yes", he looks at me and says, "Are you sure?"' The words 'are you sure' can affect a child into believing they are not trusted. The value of our words is so important in meaning what we say and saying what we mean. To be kind, generous and loving and to always see things from behind the other person's eyes, we must use our words appropriately.

The art of diplomacy is such an important one. You know they say that, for example, if your guest is leaving your house and they forget their umbrella, you will run after them and say, 'Excuse me, Sir, you forgot your umbrella?' If it's your child, your spouse or your sibling, you will say 'Ah, why did you forget your umbrella again?!' What if we were to treat everyone like a guest? To have polite behaviour towards everyone, especially those that surround us, how will it change our world? I believe that it will change our world beautifully.

Recognising the inherent value of every human life. Acknowledging our shared journey as human beings. Embracing the idea that no distinction should be made in terms of human worth. Accepting the universal reality of mortality. Appreciating the concept of karma and its potential consequences. Realising that hate is not a solution to any problem. Understanding that one's ignorance reflects solely on oneself. Acknowledging the existence of diverse perspectives in interpreting any given narrative. Recognising the significance of compassion and humanity.

The following SRT is an exercise to clear our hearts of all negativities and to turn the page, focusing on the light, letting go and giving back; leaving it all behind us until we go into depth about our relationships in Part Three.

Self-Reflective Tool 5.3: Clearing the Heart,
www.gardenofayden.com/
53clearingtheheart

ENTER THE GARDEN: MODULE 6
Pruning Of The Tree – Creating Your Vision

Purpose: We are ready to redefine ourselves. There are no limitations to what we can achieve with a balanced mindset. We define our goals with inspiration and knowledge that anything and everything is possible. We open our minds to realising the dreams of how we want to transform ourselves, who we want to be and what we want to achieve.

Branch 6.1 – The beauty of self-trust

Goal: To align what I think with what I do, to be congruent.

Duality: Fearing outcomes vs. witnessing dreams unfold.

Epiphany: I respect my past and I look forward to overcoming any obstacle with a newfound zest within me.

Affirmation: Every day, in every way, I am getting better and better.[6]

Our journey inevitably takes turns. The meaning we give to each turn depends on our character. It's our interpretation that frees or sabotages us. We all have a choice: we either doubt ourselves or we trust the journey and flow through it peacefully with grace, allowing the beauty and reward of struggle. There is a deeper sense of accomplishment and self-fulfilment. We are humble in realising how little we know, and thirsty for more. People may notice the changes without being able to pinpoint them. Is it possible to sit still, simply content, not having to prove yourself to anyone because you are comfortable within you?

A sophisticated narrative that masquerades truth cannot be blamed on the people who have been manipulated to believe it. Their reactions are understandable in their misunderstanding of what is true. Honesty requires that we untangle what the truth is rather than perpetuate violence, which is allowing puppeteers to achieve their own agenda. When we are able to raise our energy and understanding, to realise we all come from the same source, we can

---

6   É Coué, *Self-Mastery Through Conscious Autosuggestion* (American Library Service, 1922)

uphold the values that form a part of the heritage we all originate from.

They say respect is earned, a currency of actions and a testament to character. In a world where opinions clash and perspectives vary, the true challenge lies in finding common ground. It's a delicate dance between understanding, empathy and the willingness to acknowledge diverse experiences. Respect – once a straightforward concept – now weaves through the intricate threads of our interconnected lives, and yet how controversial the word now becomes. Let us navigate this complexity with open hearts, recognising that true respect is a bridge that connects us all, even in the face of disagreement.

Are you gauging that it's time to not let your past punish your present anymore, allowing yourself to stretch and remove any self-doubt? In case you were previously not being kind to yourself, you will now stop self-sabotaging, because you've replaced any doubt with positive self-belief by trusting you.

What are the new things you're looking at? How are you perceiving them? Are you able to look at yourself in the mirror and celebrate the changes you've made? What are the changes you wish to make further still?

Be honest with yourself as to what motivates you. What is it that actually makes you happy? What does happiness mean to you? There's no right or wrong in these answers. The point is to be aligned with your truths and to live them peacefully every day.

If you desire a specific outcome and are waiting for it, how is the journey of waiting? How do you speak to yourself? What do you tell yourself? Do you encourage yourself personally? Are you your best cheerleader? Are you allowing yourself to feel joyfully excited or are you scared that the outcome may be negative?

They say it's actually easier to accept negative rather than positive outcomes. We are more fearful of success than we are of failure. Why is it easier to believe something negative is happening rather than something positive? If it's because we're scared to be disappointed, wouldn't that be a pity? Isn't it better to try and fail, knowing failure doesn't exist? Every perceived failure is a sure step towards success. The learnings from each experience build our knowledge, lessons and resilience. If we do not go through the process, how may we reach our goals? We need to rise above the fear to step ahead.

Each one of us has to go through difficult experiences to stretch and grow. Many times in my own life, the negative experiences, in fact, propelled me further. They allowed me to gain confidence in seeing what I don't want.

What is it that you don't want? How are you able to let go of it peacefully? Choosing what we want is ideally based upon how we would like to spend the precious minutes of every day as opposed to a glamorous notion in our minds of an image that translates to tedious moments of execution that do not bring peace nor purpose into our daily lives. Knowing yourself helps so much in this regard and prevents so much unnecessary wasted time.

Once that peace within has settled and you are living it gracefully every day, the map becomes clearer. Our intuition awake brings us the answers effortlessly, as opposed to torturing our minds as we used to do. Getting up in the morning, knowing that we are inspired, knowing we have a purpose we want to fulfil, ideally while not being attached to the outcome, trusting that everything's happening for the highest and best reason – it's a step towards defining purpose and living our lives joyfully.

We are going forward in fulfilling our destiny, defining and living our purpose. There's an earthly purpose. There could be divine purpose, it depends on what it is for you.

What is important in this journey of your fragile life? How do you want to live it? Do you prefer to stay complaining in the mundane or do you wish to elevate yourself and say, 'All of that's in the past now'?

It would be an interesting measure to look at yourself today and see how far you have come on your journey, and you have done it yourself. All by yourself.

What I have added in the SRT for this branch is something personal and extremely close to my heart. It is all my epiphanies regarding trust while I was on my own journey that have led me here humbly in front of you to share my findings. I hope that it assists you in relieving your past and joyfully moving forward to find all your delight, with wind tickling your face, and as much contentment and peace as you may muster. I am excited for you to embrace the SRT Trust. Trust in you. Trust in others. Trust in the universe. I hope it resonates deeply within you and raises your frequency even further.

Self-Reflective Tool 6.1: Trust,
www.gardenofayden.com/61trust

Branch 6.2 – Defining my purpose

Goal: To establish who I am today and who I want to be tomorrow.

Duality: Divine light vs. stage lights.

Epiphany: I measure the fragile journey of life, knowing I am creating my vision based upon my own choices and will celebrate them every day.

Affirmation: I trust myself and know that I am able to succeed at whatever I put my heart and mind to.

What will you create to help the world and develop your legacy?

Success – however you define it – arrives when you've put in the hard work. Hard work is important. In working hard and achieving what you define as success, how do people around you react? Do you get upset because people are not validating and acknowledging you in the new things that you're doing? Do you understand why? It is not easy to see the positive outcomes of our actions in the beginning, but with persistence and perseverance we can develop ourselves and accomplish anything we put our minds to.

Remain humble. Be authentic. Be empathetic. You don't know what pain people carry that they're unable to appreciate where you are and celebrate with you. Let those feelings go. Why? Because other people are caught up with themselves, as we all are. We all go to sleep at night in our own beds. No one carries the pain we carry. We have to detach ourselves a little, because we have grown and others may not want to accept how we have changed. Don't be disappointed; it's an organic progression of life.

Rejecting prejudices and biases is the only way to attain objectivity. Without letting go of preconceived notions, our thoughts and opinions are forever coloured, and we are unable to make clear, well-informed and lucid decisions. Be proud and passionate about the things you love and believe in, the people you care about and the causes that you hold close to your heart. When you give your all to something, it creates so much energy that even a little bit of commitment and hard work goes a long way.

Please remain humble and accepting of other people's positions and stances. They need to be where they are, and you need to be where you are. You may wish to assist them. You may 'try' to assist them. Language at this stage becomes so important.

It is better to remove the word 'try' completely from your vocabulary. 'Try' allows room for failure. Therefore, we don't *try*, we *do*.

Look at how you use the word 'but'. If I say, 'I love you, but I'm angry with you', or 'I'm angry with you, but I love you', which is better? The key is to put the 'but' after the negative so that it wipes it out and the positive remains.

'Should' and 'could' are negations; use 'will' and 'do'.

How we speak to ourselves – language we use – is so important, just like the communication of the non-verbal that we talked about.

The little expressions or the way we speak to ourselves as we've deciphered makes it difficult later on if we're not aligned with ourselves.

Do you make deals with yourself or project your best outcome? Where are you now? Are you working towards your purpose? Are there stumbling blocks along the way or is it smooth sailing? Staying comfortable in discomfort, as we've talked about, allows you to keep stretching, growing and going further.

Have you defined your purpose – an earthly or divine one? How fragile this journey of ours is. What are we accomplishing for here and now, and what are we leaving behind as a legacy of something we've done as our mark of goodness? Do you ever speak to the universe? Do you ever look up to the sky and have a conversation?

By projecting the best outcome, we enhance and invigorate our journey. Man proposes and the universe disposes. If something's not right for your path, it's going to step out of your way. Believing that everything's going to happen for your highest and best paves the way for a peaceful mindset and a gentle heart rhythm. If you're still second-guessing everything and imagining the worst outcomes, you are sabotaging your potential.

Silencing the negative critic doesn't mean you are neither analysing the facts nor weighing the pros and cons. It simply means that you stop anticipating. Once satisfied with all your calculations, you let it rest. You look up to the universe and say, 'You have my back, thank you.' By engaging the universe, we bring safety to our journey, and we cease to engage in any speculation. We diminish the power of any naysayers. The simple point is, if you believe in you, it's all good.

Are you able to bring a smile to another person's face? Are you able to do something that makes you feel comfortable that you've done your part, and you are doing it quietly and discreetly? What is it that you can do to enhance someone else's life? Success depends on you, not upon the validation of others; however, serving others is relevant to your journey to maintain humility while you build success. Adding some humanity to the journey of rising and elevating is most definitely important groundwork.

May you always share your authenticity and not let success get to your head. There is neither joy nor permanence in that journey. It's key to be humble, dependable and reliable, and to share your struggles rather than boasting about your success. Allow people to understand your journey simply. They see you, they hear you and they appreciate you as you are, a down-to-earth human being, like we all are.

Integrity is defined as the quality of being honest and having strong moral principles. The state of being whole and undivided. A person with integrity behaves ethically and does the right thing, even behind closed doors. We have much work to do to bring integrity seamlessly back into our world. It is evident that the education of values is non-negotiable and an absolute and urgent necessity.

Self-Reflective Tool 6.2: A Measuring Guide,
www.gardenofayden.com/
62ameasuringguide

Branch 6.3 – Surrender and flow

Goal: To witness how a quiet mind will connect me to my deeper self and allow me to witness synchronicity.

Duality: Unknowing the known vs. knowing the unknown.

Epiphany: I am grateful every day for the beauty and inspiration in my life.

Affirmation: The silence within me holds my truth and all the answers. I allow myself to take pleasure in the unknown with trust and abandon.

We acknowledge that there is an urgency for all the old prejudices and biases to be unlearnt. We don't believe harmony is a necessity, we know it with absolute certainty. We all come from the same source, irrespective that the intentions of all may differ dramatically. Ignorance is not an excuse anymore. It is imperative we educate and allow for the freedom of all, individually and collectively.

Tying a thread of unity is not about discussion around the problem. It's about educating the people in the values that strengthen the similarities between us all and differences which are complementary if one understands the notion of one universe and one Mother Nature. Empathy and compassion must become the contemplation of accountability all around.

We disentangle ourselves from any self-limiting narrative, knowing that any situation has come to teach us something to illuminate our paths. Should we not have learnt the lesson as yet, we will continue to create similar circumstances until we reframe our position. Forgiveness is therefore not a choice as every step provides and presents an opportunity for the wisdom of the teaching to reframe itself into a blessing. Dualities are everywhere, and without them we would have no means to measure the light, hence let's embrace rather than resist them. Let's stop making the same mistakes.

When we truly awaken to the fact that this life is fragile and temporary and that we are all going to the same final destination, we establish a value of each moment of this life as precious. We let go of instant gratification, we place importance on the values that we acknowledge within and we measure each moment based upon them, rather than on the ephemeral.

We happily shoulder the duty to serve and validate others. We have no need to prove ourselves to anyone, hence we only share our thoughts through our work or when asked. We listen intently and offer our support selflessly. We feel blessed to be able to do our small part for humanity humbly.

With empathy, courage and wisdom, we continue to focus on growth and optimum development. We obliterate any form of judgement, knowing that the only way we may assist anyone else is by being an example of healthy living. We are comfortable in our skin, content with our path and wish for light upon the path of all.

We notice that when the wind blows, all the flowers and trees dance differently in the gardens and forests and create an incredible choreography of synchronicity. The uniqueness of each comes together like a melody. We embrace the eclectic nature of each of us, knowing we are all important parts of the whole, hence we flow in the festival of life.

The only thing we know is that we know nothing for sure. The minute we truly smile and accept this humbly, we stop taking ourselves so seriously. We let go of speculation and welcome the unknown. The ego washes gently away, we take a deep breath, and we watch everything with curiosity and awe. We forgive ourselves for all our complexities; we embrace them lightly and humorously and enjoy everything simply. *Carpe diem*. Wondrous wisdom.

THE HUMAN TOUCH

There is a beautiful story. A lady was in the fields working and she felt a poem coming. She went sprinting back into the house to quickly scribble down the end of the poem, then she reversed it in her mind so that she could write the whole poem because these beautiful inspirations and ideas are not available to us every minute of every day. Where do thoughts come from, and where do they go?

Every thought we have arrives from somewhere, be it the subconscious in our dreams or a fleeting moment on a quiet morning. The key is to capture all your thoughts and ideas, and not to let them pass you by. The irony is that the only way to capture them, in fact, is by letting them go, writing them down, keeping them, so that you actually remain empty to flow congruently at all times. You know that all your brilliant ideas are written down, so you have them safeguarded; that way, you can leave yourself free.

I cannot be full unless I'm empty; it's only when I am empty that I shall be full. The voice of intuition, this is the push and pull of letting oneself breathe to receive more. I remember a day when I was sitting quietly at my desk, realising that I had evolved because it was extremely busy and yet I felt totally quiet and peaceful as my lists were done. Everything that required my attention had it; all the while I had time to myself and the ability to keep my mind open and quiet.

An important part of the process is also to practise gratitude. Every day, be thankful of the little things that arrive, witness all the experiences you have and enjoy them. This allows space for abundance. It brings increased abundance. If we are not grateful for what we're receiving, how can abundance come in larger volumes? Being grateful, saying thank you to the universe every day.

There is a Wheel of Life Exercise in the following SRT to outline your journey in all aspects of your life and to keep an accountability measure for you, with you.

Self-Reflective Tool 6.3:
Wheel of Life Exercise,
www.gardenofayden.com/63wheeloflife

Transition From Part Two To Part Three

We've now completed the 'Enter the Garden' programme and walked through looking at ourselves in the mirror, using the SRTs to assist in deepening the contemplation.

Looking at the I with a Deeper Eye assists in resolving challenges we may face with others. This is an opportunity to dissolve any resentments we may carry deep within, which we may have not been able to resolve yet. The irony is that looking deeper requires a panoramic view, which means we contemplate the other's lens from each story. We desist any resistance.

Often we carry shadows of pain from past relationships, ugly divorces, parent alienation syndrome or even just a first love, a conflict with a parent, with a best friend or with workers or colleagues in the office. We often carry the guilt or the blame that can unconsciously taint our current path. Sometimes, we carry the need to be right versus doing what's right. Our cognitive biases do not help. It's a beautiful deep dive into what relationships mean. May it resolve any challenging relationship from the past or present that creates discomfort within us.

There's no point in resisting it at all. Every conflict can be solved. I say it from a position of experience in solving many a colourful conflict in the past, including my clients' conflicts too. I assure you I am not saying this off the top of my head. I know that forgiveness is the key to everything. Being able to step out of our patterns and look at things objectively is challenging yet worthy.

In case you are not a parent yourself, please know that this section will give insight into looking at your relationship with your parents and allow you to plant the seeds ahead of your journey as a parent.

Enjoy this part of the journey into exploring the intimate relationships we are all capable of having with harmony, peace and forgiveness, while respecting the knowledge that by holding onto any resentment, the only person we are hurting is ourselves.

PART THREE

LOOKING AT THE I WITH A DEEPER EYE: YOU WITH OTHERS

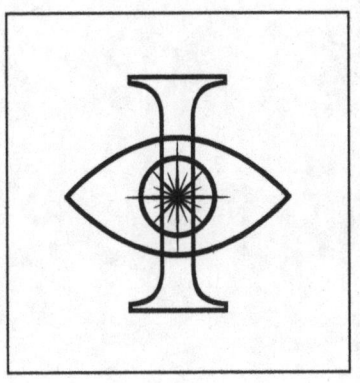

PART THREE

LOOKING AT THE I WITH A DEEPER EYE: YOU WITH OTHERS

LOOKING AT THE I WITH A DEEPER EYE: MODULE 1

Untangling Perspectives And Reframing Perceptions

Purpose: *We know that the journey has been challenging. We struggle to find our calm in the face of situations that are not only unfair but tedious and never-ending. We long for peace. We know that our intentions are good and our expectations lost. We know that to find the right outcome, we need to find our balance, first and foremost.*

Branch 1.1 – The clay half-baked or overcooked

Goal: I look for a simple understanding of what has happened without emotion, knowing this is my reality.

Duality: What was vs. what is vs. what can be.

Epiphany: I know that my truth is not anyone else's truth.

Affirmation: I make a commitment to myself to look for a way to resolve my grief.

Every situation has many imprints. What we know is a vague semblance of our own imprints; what we don't know is the other. We often don't understand how people react the way they do. We need to take a step back and humbly wonder whether everything is lost.

A bad relationship doesn't need to end in disharmony. It often happens that two good people don't get along. We always want to make one person bad, rather than accept the situation while maintaining respect. Are we willing to validate ourselves or do we have regrets? Are we able to calm down, take a look in the mirror and see things differently? Many times, in the anguish of loss, we want to react immediately or numb the pain and apply a plaster rather than allow a wound to breathe.

Every person's situation and circumstances are different, yet we can find commonalities that may bridge our understanding together. Misunderstandings, misjudgements, a malice of intent, malevolence – ignorance is never an excuse for bad behaviour. Let's grant the benefit of the doubt and generosity at the offset. Let's believe that everyone is capable of change.

It is a big leap towards an open mind and the healthiest first step we can take.

We are all guilty of misdemeanours. Like it or not, we all make mistakes. The crazy part is that we look at other people's mistakes as being unacceptable, yet we are not accountable for our own. The first culprit is usually the ego; the second is dodging the responsibility. Hence when communication fails dramatically, we resort to blame, to judge and to be unforgiving.

When we want goodness and yet we're punishing someone, giving them grief, we know that we will not accomplish the outcome we seek. When we know that our intentions are clear and we have forgiven ourselves, can we not forgive someone else? If we take a step back, bite our tongues, struggle with ourselves, we can find a place of peace. Where we are able to lift our eye and say, 'I was wrong too. It's not only the other person that made mistakes because I made mistakes as well.'

We cover all the different situations where we have disagreements. For example, someone spoke too badly and you responded badly; it's created a rift. The first question is: is it your ego that's going to say, 'No, I'm not asking for forgiveness' or can you sit back and say, 'You know what, I value this relationship. I do want it to work, and I will not let my ego get in the way because the relationship has value to me.'

Let's look at the situation as it stands peacefully, quietly, and without emotion, and question the collateral damage. What has happened up until now? Let's look at it without any emotion with a cold eye. If you value a relationship, letting it go because of ego, not wanting to be wrong, or someone's made you feel bad doesn't make sense. It's more valuable to be open, see where the pieces fall and let the dust settle.

Allow yourself to feel what you feel, hear what you hear, see what you see. Forgive yourself. Accept the discomfort, any jealousy, hatred, deceit, whatever happened as being what it is. It is what it is. Thereafter we can ponder with a fresh eye. 'Has the person deceived me, or did I deceive myself by trusting too much?' Did I put my boundaries down, or is it because the other person has different boundaries? There are always two people with two characters and two perspectives.

Each person will reframe perspectives differently because they have a different baseline, a different education. What they perceive as normal and what you perceive as normal are completely different. We unconsciously believe the other person is wrong because they do not think like we do. What if we are to take the view of the other person and look at it from behind their eyes? If we're feeling frustrated, we may feel there's been deceit; we may feel betrayed. We feel our boundaries invaded. We accept it, we accept everything we're feeling, we allow ourselves to feel it and yet keep it cold.

Keeping it cold rationalises a situation, especially when strong emotions are involved. We can find emotional logic. We untangle the pieces to question: 'If I am jealous, could it be because I'm insecure and uncomfortable in my skin?' Jealousy is not a valuable asset. What can we hold ourselves accountable for? What are we responsible for?

Once the emotions have calmed down, we can be honest with ourselves. We need to separate the theatre of our imagination from what is factually true because we may be hurting and yet still love someone deeply. Often we make the mistake of letting go simply because we're hurting, rather than looking for balance, without realising we may still hurt if they're gone.

Resentment only hurts you. It does not hurt the other person. They can carry on with their lives. Holding any resentment within you only hurts you. There are often complications we create that we haven't even perceived yet. If we leave no other choice but elegance, it will reign. Playing judge and jury achieves nothing because our opinion is not more important than any other. Man is equal. Yes, the size of people's hearts are most definitely different. Values are different. If we've been hurt, there may be a hidden blessing for our growth, which we may have even created subconsciously.

The affirmation of this branch is: I make a commitment to myself to look for a way to resolve my grief. Sitting as victims doesn't suit us, and there's no reason why we have to remain so. Let's make the commitment to resolve any grief that lingers within. Being able to step out of our patterns and look at things objectively is challenging but worthy.

Imagine this as a metaphor in any situation. You take a chandelier of any relationship, and you just smash it. It's impossible to put the pieces back together. Alternatively, when you dismantle the chandelier piece by piece, polish the individual crystals and carefully put them back, it has so much more value. Healing is possible when we untangle the pieces and look at them objectively from a distance. Assuming a little responsibility brings humility and carves the path towards our freedom of spirit.

Branch 1.2 – Dancing with discomfort

Goal: To understand it is not about who was right; it is about my boundaries being protected.

Duality: Ruled by my emotions vs. ruled by my heart.

Epiphany: Each person has their own understanding of what boundaries are, and this does not make me wrong.

Affirmation: I understand that each person lives in a different reality.

It's not about who was right and who was wrong. It's about protecting boundaries and respecting each other. We sometimes want to punish the other person, so we say things we don't mean and they say things they don't mean, then we end up in a deadlock of a situation where each person wants to be stubborn. Each one of us has different stories in our minds depending on how we have defined the narrative.

How can we be understood precisely and accurately? How can we find a way that people understand exactly what we mean and what we think? The game of 'he said, she said' distorts things so fast, and we get blamed for things just because it's taken out of context, which happens so often.

How can we feel understood simply? Are we delivering our truth or are we protecting ourselves with our ego? The framework of ego doesn't suit us and habitually brings the wrong response. If I say what I mean and I mean what I say, I will be understood simply. If I'm angry, it's better that I don't say anything until I have calmed down and I'm able to look at things objectively. It's always about keeping that cognitive eye high to see things from a peak mountaintop position that brings us distance from the actual situation.

Am I behaving the way that actually brings me what I want? I know that the answer is often 'no' while sitting at the top of the mountain because I want peace and joy. I'm kicking up a fuss and creating nonsense, because I want to punish the other person for hurting me.

Did the other person hurt me, or did I hurt myself because of my reaction? Did the other person hurt me, or did I misconstrue their words and intent? Did I misinterpret? Did I trigger them?

Let's step out of the context of situations and look at it objectively. Start with the basics. What do I want to achieve? What is my goal? Am I angry? Do I want to let a situation go, even though there's love in my heart, or am I happy to let it go because I know it's for my highest and best?

Contemplate from a frame of mind of achieving the best outcome for all. Am I able to discern what I am willing to accept and what is non-negotiable? Am I able to make a list of values I wish to live by? If the other person can accept these, then everything is fine. If it's going against my values, I can make a list of things that need to be amended, with a peaceful mind, to look for agreement.

It's a battle of many stages, and we have to go through the different stages to find truths. Are you willing, or are you going to hold tight and say, 'No, I'm right, and I want to be right'? It's worth a think.

Clarifying truths is more important than who was right and who was wrong. As I said, the 'he said, she said' doesn't help us. Perhaps you want to stay in a drama within yourself because you believe you were treated so badly. A clarification of this is in the detail of 'how I feel' rather than 'this is how *you* made me feel'.

People may communicate badly and still have the best of intentions. People who communicate well may have bad intentions. We don't know. We can never see a person's intention. If our intuition is clear, we may feel things deeply, but we don't know for sure. Are you able to allow the benefit of the doubt and give a person some space to contemplate whether you were wrong in your judgements and to see them from a different eye?

You have loved the person before. If they were your best friend, spouse, parent or sibling and today you see them differently, are you able to give them back the eye that you had on them before, all the while forgiving them for whatever has happened, knowing that you are partly responsible? It's a worthy journey to do, and I hope that you will take the time to conclude that you can do this. I'm able to grant my highest and best to everyone involved.

We create better understanding and clarity in our communications by acknowledging and accepting the boundaries and beliefs of each other and deriving a consensus through active listening and effective communication. The way we perceive a situation decides its outcome. Hindsight makes us realise that the changes we dreaded ultimately led to something better than we had imagined. Instead of resisting change, we recognise the unexpected as a virtue. When we change the way we look at things, the things we look at change. We are responsible for the choices we make. Life brings us new choices every day, and it is up to us to make the right ones.

We often mismanage situations, allowing them to create more trouble for ourselves by questioning other people's mistakes rather than humbly observing our own. When we decide to blame, judge and be unforgiving, we are creating distance. Let's dissolve any conflict by perceiving every moment through the eye of compassion.

Branch 1.3 – Secrets and sacrifices

Goal: To measure if my words and actions always accurately represent my heart and mind.

Duality: Complaining, criticising, comparing vs. conscious, compassionate, complete.

Epiphany: It is so easy to be misunderstood. I didn't know I was until I saw it in the response received.

Affirmation: I will make an effort to precisely say what I mean and mean what I say.

What secret are you holding, and what sacrifices are you making? We often sacrifice our truths, and hold our secrets close to our chests, thinking it will protect us and protect our relationship with others. It's quite the contrary because the minute we're holding secrets within us, we will become suspicious, believing other people are holding secrets within them. We tend to always project our inner feelings on to others.

If you're not living with your authenticity, you will quickly suppose other people are not being authentic. Are we wearing masks, or are we being true to ourselves? If we're being true to ourselves, are we being true to others around us? It's easy for us to blame other people for things that we are guilty of ourselves. If we don't hold ourselves accountable, how can we expect other people to be accountable to us?

Peeling off the layers is being able to look in the mirror with purity and truth. If we've been sacrificing truth or hiding secrets, we need to come to terms with it being wrong. It's understandable if there is no desire to create more trouble by sharing truths now. Admitting hard truths brings humility and the ability to forgive ourselves. This can sometimes be the most important part of the journey because we hate ourselves when we are resistant to our own faults. Forgiving ourselves gives space and brings relief. Acknowledging truths that are challenging creates the shifts.

Living with half-truths forces other people to live with half-truths as well. We want to blame or criticise them, or we feel like there's an elephant in the room. Why does this happen? Because we're not actually living genuinely, mind, heart, body and soul together as one person aligned. If we're aligned, we can find our truths in simplicity, and we can make the right decisions congruently.

For us to justify noise in our minds about other people, we have to first see what we're guilty of and then take a good look in the mirror. You know the detail of any specific situation better than I do because it's your situation. My suggestion is to hash out that detail, zoom into it deeply to find the mirror where you admit what you're guilty of, first and foremost to yourself. You with you. Should you be willing, undo the narrative that is holding you hostage to release any resentment from your heart. Resentment serves no one.

Is it fair to punish your heart or the heart of another? If I'm insecure, is it fair that I make someone else feel bad for that? Or is it my responsibility to feel self-secure to withstand and sustain any situation that arises? Often, our demons are our own and yet we blame them on other people. It's not fair. We're not allowed to do that. It doesn't work. Let's resolve our own challenges first and admit our misdemeanours. Once we're honest with ourselves, we can measure the other person's reactions more precisely. We may actually have sympathy and empathy because it's possible we suddenly realise that the other has been pristine in their management of us.

I didn't know I wasn't at peace until I was. It's a beautiful line. I didn't know I wasn't at peace because I was busy fighting with myself. The minute I liberated that, the minute I liberated the noise and comforted myself, I was able to find peace. Why? Because I'm not demanding something from somebody else. I'm not seeking someone else to make me feel better about me. It's me who has to make me feel better about me. I don't need to wait for someone to buy me roses, I buy my own roses, and you should too.

What is the demand that we have? Why do we feel that to be loved, someone has to do A, B or C for us, be it a parent, a friend, a spouse or a partner? One has to take responsibility and accountability for oneself to be happy. Have I shared with my loved ones and my spouse the way I became who I am today? Have I told my parents my experiences that I had at school or university that shaped the way I am today? Have I described to those people that count, the noises that I have in my mind and the way I speak to myself?

We are one human being, and our relationships with each person in our lives are limited when we are actually so complete. Wanting balance is to be in relationships where we are safe to be expansive authentically and aligned with our truths. How many of us hold this as our measure? It's the path to our natural harmony. A beautiful one. A worthy one. Before we want to blame someone else for our situation, individually or collectively, we must first look at ourselves. We can estimate whether we've been responsible in sharing, in being authentic, in being loving. We can then look at whether the situation right now has been caused by doubt, insecurity or jealousy. To really name it, call it what it is, and learn to say what you mean and mean what you say.

LOOKING AT THE I WITH A DEEPER EYE: MODULE 2
The Desire To Be Deserving

Purpose: We are contemplating what it means to be loving and to be loved. We are defining what we believe this means and if our definition matches the life we have lived, and, if it doesn't, seeking to understand why not.

Branch 2.1 – The rose and the thorn

Goal: To set the stage of how I made the choices that I did.

Duality: Narrative vs. truth.

Epiphany: Context plays an incredible role in who I become.

Affirmation: I shall set a vision of how I would like to live, and my path will change.

An old Persian proverb says, 'He who wants the rose, needs to be able to withstand the thorns.'[7] Are we demanding and expecting love without questioning how much we're giving? Are we being demanding without understanding our need to participate and reciprocate? What is it that we seek, and why are we entitled to receive without giving?

When we look in the mirror, we ensure that we are actually fulfilling our role of providing those that are under our care with that nurturing. It could even be in the office. As CEO, are you providing your employees their well-being and security to be deserving of it in return? Life is all about balance, which is often lacking. Striking the balance of give and take to create a happy marriage or a healthy business relationship. Harmony cannot be achieved if it's one person who's benefiting and the other person losing out. It's obvious, yet how many of us actually follow this?

Where is the onus of responsibility? What changes when the onus is solely ours? As we know from Enter the Garden, responsibility is the ability to respond appropriately. Let's ask ourselves if we have given from the heart generously. If the answer is yes, we can question ourselves from the eyes of the other person to understand why they treat us in this way. What motivation could they have to be difficult with us? Is there something that we're missing? Is there something that we didn't do?

---

7   Author unknown, origin unknown.

Humility demands that we ask ourselves the right questions. Humility demands that we ask the other person the same questions. Being authentic, honest and vulnerable is a journey towards alignment and finding your truths. We carry the fragments of our past within us. We carry our previous challenges too, unless we have untangled ourselves deeply as we are doing here. Should we measure someone in front of us today using the fragments of our past, we will continue to make the same mistakes. We consciously recognise that our past will not punish our present. It's wrong. It's unfair. We need to be careful not to repeat these stories in our minds which are extremely unhealthy for us. We are all human. We all make mistakes. Let's be able to take a new conversation forward; a new conversation that involves holding boundaries – yours and the other person's boundaries. Respecting that the other person has different desires to yours. Respecting that if you want to be in a relationship with someone, you have to be able to see life from behind their eyes and match it, or else that's not a relationship. It's tyrannical.

What changes could we have made to not reach this dire situation? Could we have spoken differently? Could we have understood something differently? Finding truth requires vulnerability. Vulnerability is strength; we know that. Vulnerability is being able to look at another person, take responsibility and apologise. You misunderstood me, and I misunderstood you. Can we look at a way of resolving this peacefully for the best interest of all involved?

Members of a family often break up, and it's the children that suffer. Friends break up, and if part of a group of friends, the whole group suffers. At work, same issue. We assume responsibility and accountability for those we affect who suffer for our mistakes. How can a person we once loved cause so much anguish? Love and hate are intertwined; it's indifference that is the opposite of love, not hatred. If we're indifferent, we don't care. We have no feeling. Hence hatred spells some kind of attachment. It's a juxtaposition. Let us all live our lives peacefully by being fair, honest, congruent, transparent.

We know that human nature is constantly evolving. Nothing is stagnant in the world. As we grow, as we develop, relationships develop. They transform, they change, and we are always sharing responsibility to create the best outcome for all around us. Efforts are a constant necessity. A relationship is hard work. It takes two to tango, as they say. If we've become complacent or lazy or we're feeling bad within ourselves, it is not fair to take it out on the other person. We stay on our tiptoes, on our best behaviour at all times.

Our laziness is not a good reason for a rift. Even when we're distracted or busy at work and the other person is being demanding. Are we responding or reacting? Are we validating the other and apologising for our lack of attention or are we getting triggered and making matters worse? A healthy apology is made in three steps:

1. I'm sorry.
2. It will never happen again.
3. What can I do to make it up to you?

It is not muttering a disgruntled apology under our breath and being annoyed if the other person is not happy with it.

Taking away the ego from the communication is a big step. Are we unconsciously punishing the other person, pretending to be angry just to get more attention? A diva sequence is called secondary gain. It is deceitful and dishonest. Secondary gain is when a person who received attention because of a misfortune or illness continues the same drama to receive more attention. Demanding attention using emotional bribery and guilt cannot bring love. We have to be fair in the way we treat other people. The Golden Rule: treat unto others as you would want them to treat you.[8] It stands true.

Feeling justified in bad behaviour because we are mistreated could be why values are lacking in today's world. Should everyone follow this logic, the frequency of our planet is obviously unkind and

---

8 J Wattles, *The Golden Rule* (Oxford University Press, 1996)

selfish. Being willing to acknowledge and accept our mistakes can work wonders. There is a disclaimer of coming into awareness, so amends are possible. Regret is useless. Are we able to simply make amends and wash away the hurt? We cannot carry on with our mistakes and turn a blind eye with no regret. We have to make amends and clean the slate. Crying over spilled milk is useless.

Why not give the other person a chance as well? Give the other person a chance to breathe peacefully. Allow a dialogue. Allow breathing space. Allow yourself to sit in front of the other person without judgement and observe where they're coming from. Feel their energy. What is fascinating as the facts evolve and as we evolve, the truth often changes too. As we take distance from a situation, we can see it from so many different eyes. Giving us space and a chance to breathe into bringing peace back to a relationship, as opposed to judging it, blaming it, playing judge and jury.

Branch 2.2 – The juxtaposition of joy vs. jealousy

Goal: To understand that I set myself up in bringing truth to my projections.

Duality: Eyes of beholder vs. judgemental gaze.

Epiphany: The only person I can control is myself.

Affirmation: I will give space to those I love to be who they are.

We set ourselves up with the projections of what we expect to happen rather than allowing our loved ones the space to be themselves. By us taking this position or stance, we stunt growth. We jeopardise authenticity.

Sadly, we often miscalculate our self-worth and subconsciously judge ourselves. We give away our power without even being aware of it. When we are living from our highest and best, however other people are treating us, we know that this is their problem, not ours. We are secure in the self-knowledge that we are living to our highest of values, consciously having done the work, and not because of any ego illusions.

If we, in our intentions, have messed up or are angry, and we want to hurt someone, the bottom line is about our own mirror. With our map now polished, there is no way the other person will treat us badly. If they do, we can clearly discern their intentions, and distance ourselves effortlessly. We have to be able to treat ourselves and everyone around us well to breed positive, harmonious results.

Fear risks becoming our worst enemy without the coping skills to manage situations. Circumstantial trauma is what happens when an unexpected situation arises. It is up to us to seek out the coping skills necessary. We have the possibility to create any outcome we want by pursuing our highest and best standards at all times.

Tell me it's impossible to do? No, it's not. It's hard work we all deserve for our own sake and for the sake of our families, our children, all of our loved ones. If we are not putting in the effort, who else will?

If we become victims of circumstance, what happens? Nothing happens. We end up in a negative spiral. Taking the possibility that there is a positive interpretation to any situation is the birthplace of faith. If we are listening for the clues that the universe wishes to feed us, it gives us the possibility to imagine different outcomes with the people that we are struggling with because we're leaving them room to breathe. We invite the opportunity for them to become wholesome with us. We must seek the right results to invite them. It starts with us.

If I am angry, daily events become turbulent and unmanageable. Remember the coping mechanism from Enter the Garden with our fingers and toes as air valves, where no emotion, frustration or stress can get stuck within the body. We are breathing freely, and once the flow is mastered, our viewpoints change.

We project positively and give another person the benefit of the doubt. It changes everything. It's like the pink sunglasses. We mend whatever we like in our life. The challenge is the victim mindset. If you still feel like someone has wronged you, pause, breathe and think again. See it from a different eye and see what changes.

Ask yourself:

- Had my behaviour been different, could things have been different?
- If I had given love rather than waiting to receive love, could things have been different?
- If I had been loving rather than jealous, could things have been different?
- If I had given the other person a chance, could things have been different?

There are many questions we have to ask ourselves to go deeper and deeper into resolving these topics without any regret. We are simply aligning our accountability to no longer repeat the same mistakes.

Do we give the eye of attention to whether someone is deserving of our love, or do we give the eye of attention if we deserve their love? It's a good question to ask yourself. Which eye are you looking at it from? Are you looking from behind the other person's eye, or are you looking at it from behind your eye with insecurity?

If you're looking at it from behind your eye with love, generosity, grace and humility, you're able to achieve anything you want. If you're proud, angry and stuck in your ego, thinking that showing vulnerability, love or care may portray you as weak, think again. Love is about being unconditional. Sadly, there are so many people who think love is conditional. 'I will love you if you do this' is just wrong. It's completely wrong.

What we are talking about here is our humility and our high standards. It's all about being humble with high standards. Being low maintenance, taking away expectations and giving freely of ourselves. Being able to give generously, even if someone doesn't love us back in the first instance. It doesn't work to secretly love someone but continue to treat them badly and expect them to come back gracefully. It doesn't work like that. Vulnerability is the key to strength. Accepting situations for what they are, as they are right now, and breathing deeply.

Branch 2.3 – The ability to forgive everything, knowing it takes two to tango

Goal: I know that I am not a perfect human being, as no one is.

Duality: Enthused vs. deflated.

Epiphany: I forgive myself for my shortcomings.

Affirmation: All the weeds are vanishing from my conscience and spirit.

THE DESIRE TO BE DESERVING

We know that none of us are perfect human beings. We may like to believe we are perfect while maintaining the belief that everyone else is at fault. It doesn't work. We have to treat everyone with the same fragility as we want them to treat us with. If we focus on our own standards, we give everyone else the ability to raise theirs. If we are setting high standards for ourselves while accepting nothing less than those high standards, we give the opportunity of growth to all. We may even teach by way of example by being forgiving and offering empathy to all. Opening the door to the benefit of doubt with wisdom as our guide.

Remember the example of the thirteen-year-old and three-year-old and expecting something impossible. Metaphorically speaking we know this applies to all of us. We are all on the same journey, at different stations in our understanding, awareness, skill sets and characters. We cannot be unforgiving because of character or behaviour differences. Tolerance is our duty. Wisdom breeds patience. We reframe our frustration, seeing the three-year-old as endearing.

As wise and understanding teachers, we don't nag; we live by way of example, modelling the behaviour we wish to see. We see life from behind their eyes, understand it, walk next to them, hand in hand from their perspective to the vision we wish them to perceive. No expectation of outcome. Delicately and gently, to achieve harmony and peace. Unconditional love requires forgiveness, not standing guard, not holding blame. When we indulge in blaming others, we give away our power and our strength. There's no other way about it. How much are you blaming? How much are you holding other people responsible? What can you do to change that?

There is so much you can do. Just see it from a different eye. Expand your horizon. Look at it differently. If I feel entitled to believe that I deserve what I deserve, I'm shooting myself in the foot because I'm stamping my feet, and I'm saying, 'No, I want it, but I'm not willing to work for it.' How can that be? Is it fair? Is that the right way to handle other people, or is it better to allow yourself to be flexible and dance in the wind?

Reacting is spur of the moment. Responding is an art. We take all the information with an open mind. We mull it over, we contemplate it, we look to understand where the other person is coming from. Once we have understood their perspective, we respond warmly, with empathy and unconditional love. We generously give them the benefit of the doubt. It works.

If we live without expectations, we can always be surprised at the kindness of other human beings. We'll be constantly surprised when anyone is nice to us because we expect nothing. Its lovely, because every day, we have these beautiful little surprises. It's when we are holding expectations that we will always be disappointed. Why are we not allowing other people to live the way they feel? Why are we wanting to put them in a box? We end up suffocating them.

Disappointment is the dance between our expectations and the gift of the truth we feed ourselves. If we allow ourselves to dance freely, we will always be content, happy and peaceful because we will watch everything that's happening around us as if it's magic, neither wishing to control nor demand anything. I'm not asking anyone to behave the way I want them to. I'm letting them be them, and I will be me, at my highest and best.

The journey from selfishness to selflessness is such an interesting one and can be quite entertaining too. The minute we understand the concept and notice where we are acting selfishly, we feel almost embarrassed within. This painlessly creates the opening to be softer with ourselves, while making the necessary adjustments in our behaviour as it has become so blatantly obvious to us. There is no return to misaligned behaviour once understood.

Do you feel selfless or selfish by nature? If I'm selfish and looking after myself to be good for those I love, that's fine. Being selfish and demanding, I'm taking goodness away. Selflessness means giving other people the same grace that I give myself – being surprised, aware and alert to the small, beautiful nuances.

Live with appreciation in each moment. How many of us constantly presume the negative and, in turn, create reactions that blatantly demonstrate the negativity in our eyes, faces and demeanour. We wonder about the reaction we receive, while perhaps being oblivious to what has invited the response. It's all about an open disposition. We give to receive. If we're not giving, we cannot expect to receive.

Do you feel that you are slowly detaching all the triggers that you have to invite peace? Be generous in allowing people to be who they are, to come to you peacefully and sweetly with love.

Remember, all that anybody wants is to be validated, to be loved, to be accepted. We all go screaming and shouting, thinking that we're not being loved while not giving any love. Let's give before we receive and know that we will receive by giving.

LOOKING AT THE I WITH A DEEPER EYE: MODULE 3

The Constant Evolution Of Our Person

Purpose: We know that nothing remains stagnant or constant. It is a journey and not a destination. Our impressions are in perpetual transition. When we accept this as a reality, we gain the ability to be flexible in the snapshots we take in our minds and allow for a moving picture that we learn to enjoy with its ups and downs, while keeping a keen eye on our intentions.

Branch 3.1 – The flexibility of my impressions

Goal: To become my own encouraging taskmaster and my best friend.

Duality: Mystery of life vs. slave to the ego.

Epiphany: Not every one of my thoughts has to be carved in stone. I, too, can be wrong.

Affirmation: I allow myself to stretch and stretch further to encompass and embrace new perspectives of myself.

Here we are asking ourselves how we perceive life. If we allow for a moving reality, in every moment, things change. It forces us to relinquish control. We all think we're in control but we're actually not.

Are the impressions that we're holding agitating our minds? Are we measuring everything against the agitation in our minds, or are we allowing people to flow freely? Are we letting go of overthinking and being oversensitive to the behaviour of others in situations we cannot control?

There's a lovely story of two monks. They are walking by a lake, when they see a lady. She requests if one of them could carry her over the lake. The taller monk replies positively, elegantly lifts her safely over his shoulder and they proceed to cross the lake. When they reach the other side, she humbly expresses her gratitude, and they continue on their way. Two hours later, the shorter monk turns to him and says, 'I can't believe you carried that lady.' The taller monk looks at him with a gentle smile and replies, 'I left her at the edge of the lake two hours ago. Why are you still carrying her?'

The moral of the story is that any agitation we carry belongs only to us. We may be grieving over something that has no relevance to the misinterpreted, the trouble is within us and has nothing to do with their intentions. The tall monk's intention was to be helpful; he carried the lady out of the kindness of his heart with no malevolent intention. The shorter monk carried the agitation for two hours prior to criticising the taller monk. There was no purpose to his agitation except for being extremely judgemental of the taller monk based upon his own sceptical mindset.

We have to question ourselves. We have to measure what we are holding and what we decide to release and let go of. What are we secretly blaming on other people without them even knowing? When we're measuring every aspect of life against that, is it fair to you or the other person? Is it accurate, or is it your cognitive bias of wanting to be right, therefore you're measuring everything in the negative?

Life is a constantly evolving movie that we witness. We don't want to hold on too tight and we refrain from our judgemental narrative wishing to label, box and shelve topics or people to make ourselves feel more secure that we understand. This creates the unease within us, because we think we are safer if we can define things. It requires courage to allow the flow. We allow for fleeting moments that we gaze upon with curiosity without overanalysing. The meaning will always reveal itself when needed. We enjoy every moment for what it is. Should something negative happen, we can simply look up at the sky and wonder what the universe is doing without overthinking it, allowing ourselves to flow, with respect of the understanding that we control nothing.

Are you superficial and joyful with society but then mean and miserable with those you love? How do you interact with people at work? Do you have empathy for them? Do you look at life from behind their eyes and see what they're going through? Are you grateful, or are you thinking the grass is greener on the other side? Do you feel only your life is more important than anyone else's? How can that be joyful if you don't even give grace and empathy for other people's woes, let alone those closest to you?

We punish the people closest to us the most because we take them for granted. Why do we take them for granted when they're the most precious things to us? We should be in gratitude twenty-four seven for those closest to us and express that gratitude with love, generosity and happiness. Making them feel good, not waiting for them to make us feel good. Am I the sum of what everybody thinks of me, or do I have my own honourable impressions about myself? How important is what other people think of me?

Are you able to let go of other people's impressions and be authentically you to do what's right, while giving of yourself generously? I invite you to do that contemplation. It's a worthy one. Refrain from holding any impressions of anything or anyone. Be a blank canvas. Just be selfless and give of yourself.

What relationships will you change when you do that? Who will you seek forgiveness from? Who will you call to check if they're OK? What would you do differently if you're forgetting about you? You only focus your attention on making other people happy. Which wrongs would you want to make right? Are there any?

What words are you using that other people will take graciously? In my actions, in my communication, is my awareness at its best or am I living inside my head, only thinking about me? Am I generous of heart? What is my motivation, in my words, in my actions? What is my intention?

Self-accountability is the yardstick. We talk about it, and we'll keep talking about it. Self-accountability is about stopping with the take, take, take and the me, me, me. Looking outward and saying, 'Have I given my best?' If the answer is 'yes', your world is blissful and peaceful. This is validation for you. If the answer is 'no', I urge you to please go within. Don't look outside for answers. Only look to yourself and to see what you can change within because you can change your world and the world of everyone around you. Be free, be generous, be liberated. Let it go.

Branch 3.2 – Is a mistake a misery or a miracle?

Goal: To understand there can be good in what I immediately deem as bad, just as there can be trouble in what I see as beautiful.

Duality: Roller coaster emotions vs. stable heart.

Epiphany: I take distance to re-evaluate what was and what is, and joy in knowing what might be.

Affirmation: The minute I can perceive duality in different moments, I feel wisdom becoming my companion.

Often what we deem as good turns into bad, and what we deem as troublesome turns into a miracle and goodness for us. Being able to measure the dualities of life and understand that sometimes our impressions can change, depending on the moment, is the birthplace of wisdom.

Wisdom becomes our companion to understand that the same task or situation can be good or bad for us, depending on how we perceive and handle it and on the outcome. If we deem it bad because we expected a different outcome but we have a miracle from it, then it's a blessing. Which eye are you giving to things? This is a time to take distance to re-evaluate the gains and the losses.

What do you deem as a gain and what do you deem as a loss? How are you measuring it? Against what? Do you see the goodness that comes out of situations that were deemed as bad? Do you see the wisdom you have gained? Are you appreciating even the good that comes out of bad situations? Are you able to measure it and say, 'Yes, thank you, it's been beautiful'?

Whereas everybody's looking at it as a disaster for you, you're actually appreciating the beauty of what you gained from it. It's worth a challenge to see what you can appreciate, even in the bad moments.

Look at Cinderella's journey.[9] Is her fate terrible? Was she negative because of her wicked stepmother, or did she help out as much as she could? Would she still have gained the love of the prince if she had a negative character? Is her journey ending beautiful or terrible? She married the prince, while she had a terrible childhood. A good outcome came from a bad situation. If Cinderella had been resentful and wicked, what good would have come of it? Nothing. Could she have wanted to change her fate or do something differently? Or was she accepting of it and happy knowing that she had jealous people around her? If she made mistakes, did she beat herself up, or did she accept them willingly, grow from them and become humbler?

---

9   J Grimm, and W Grimm, *Grimm's Fairy Tales* (various publishers, 1812)

Cinderella's story can help a lot of us to figure out mistakes made and things gained. It's worth looking at. It's a childhood legend, and it's something that carries a lot of weight if we look at it from the right eye. If we want other people to forgive our mistakes, are we able to forgive theirs?

What is this journey of forgiveness? What does it require? Does it require you going backwards and seeing the things you did but actually being able to see it from the eye of the other person? Are you able to look at things differently, to know that you can let go? You can allow what was to be and then look forward to what might be in the future.

Accepting our past and everything that's happened, with all the mistakes we made, is a step towards happiness, peace and joy. Holding demons holds no value. What if someone doesn't know that you consider that they've made a mistake? What if they can't understand how you're perceiving something because they were brought up with different values? What if they can't get the point you're trying to make of what you deem as right?

Not because they don't care and they have bad intentions but because they just don't have the same DNA, the same values, the same education. They function from their mind rather than from their heart, from their logic rather than their empathy. Maybe you're holding bad intentions but they are not. Are they free in their belief? You're treating them badly based on what you think, rather than opening your third eye. Call it what you like, it's the I of the deeper eye. See what you could do differently in your thought processes to invite forgiveness and allow yourself – rather force yourself – to try and perceive something from someone else's perspective, a completely different perspective. You can welcome it because all of us are unique, and all of us are different.

No two people function the same way. People don't function the way we do. What if you could turn the eye and say, 'It's actually my duty to try and figure out the logic behind that person's perspective. It's my duty to figure out their thought process and understand it from their eye, not from mine. Remove my eye completely and see it from theirs.'

As a first task, that would be amazing in terms of bridging things together. If you're able to recognise that you do not agree with a standpoint but understand it, the journey towards validation has begun. That's enabling a voice, allowing the other to have a different opinion than you do; even if you don't like it, you can accept it. That's what boundaries are about.

Pain allows us to appreciate life so much more. People who have not gone through any hazardous situations don't understand the value of the little things. It's only when people have lost something that they appreciate its value. When you take pain as a measure of bliss, joy and gratitude, and you say to yourself, 'It's by going through pain that I am a more wholesome person', it actually makes you more generous, more forgiving, more open and more welcoming rather than closed and resentful.

Take every bad experience you've had as a beautiful lesson to make you a bigger person, to make you a more wholesome person, to appreciate the nuances and the depth of life. Every moment counts.

Did you imagine your today to look the way it does, or did you imagine it differently? Can you perceive it differently again tomorrow? Can you improve on your today? What is holding you back? What is stopping you? What is it that you can do to make it better, proactively with generosity today?

Branch 3.3 – Retrospect is respect for what was

Goal: By reflecting on the beauty that was, I may make peace with what is today.

Duality: Discernment vs. discrimination.

Epiphany: I no longer hold on to resentment that was only causing me anguish.

Affirmation: I can appreciate and celebrate every crossroad in my journey because they have made me who I am today.

By measuring the beauty of what was, I see it differently today. I make peace knowing that resentment was harming me. I will care enough for myself to heal. No point holding on to old resentments. I can celebrate every crossroad because it created the person I am today. Our minds can be sometimes cruel, turning the romantic story into a saga or drama. If we play these stories to ourselves over and over, deciding to feel 'woe is me' rather than contemplate correction, it becomes a vicious cycle.

When, in sessions, I request couples to reflect back to when Cupid hit, they both recall happy memories, shifting their energy in that same moment. We have to be so careful in how we discipline our minds.

We also need to be cautious of the context that surrounds certain decisions we make. We may be feeling lonely or unwell. We decide to engage for the wrong reasons, because of loneliness rather than that person being right for us. We all make mistakes of all types.

Can we measure the distance, remembering the person we were then and the person we've become? Can we find that balance between all the elements and the why?

Do we change perspective the minute we have something we thought we wanted when buying something new? We wear it for a few days, and then forget about it. It doesn't stay new. Are we the same in handling our relationships? Have we boxed something, ribboned it, put it on a shelf and concluded what it means, while keeping the same impressions? We've changed too. What are the truths of who we were then, how the other person evolved and who we are today? What does that journey look like? How do you measure it? Are you giving it grace? Can you give it more grace?

We attract whatever we are at each stage of our journey. You will notice that people enter and exit your life at different periods because your energies are different. You will attract what is similar to you.

Appreciating what we attract means looking back at ourselves, the I of the deeper eye into self-accountability. When I want to attract something differently, it's my energy that must change first.

We get what we deserve. We decide what we deserve and invite it, by doing the search within, without assigning blame. When we seek solace and decide to forgive, we invite a refreshing story and create something a lot more evolved, a lot wiser. We reframe our past with wisdom and alter the erroneous narrative with grace and humility. Do you have the humility to be able to do that? Do you believe it?

When we're cruel and mean to another human being, the only person we end up hating is ourselves. We punish people, yet we don't like ourselves for doing it and we think it's beyond us to avoid it. It's untrue. Behave as you would want to receive love. Good behaviour invites a good feeling; bad behaviour invites anguish. Let's let go of the pain, lift ourselves out of it, forgive ourselves for indulging in hurting other people. Let's start liking ourselves again. After liking ourselves, then we can go and talk to the person who hurt us, forgive them and apologise: 'I acted badly. I was in pain. It happens. Please forgive me. It won't happen again. What can I do to make it up to you?'

You know, the possibilities are vast if we allow them to be. How's your ego doing now? Do you feel like staying in your ego? Do you want to keep it some more? For what value? What will you gain? You'll be the loser at the end of it. You are not your story, and your story is not you. You have every wholesome piece inside of you to rebuild, reframe, restructure and re-engage. You have all the reasons to make everything right.

Why keep pain and loss? Why inflict outcomes on other people that they don't deserve? It's not fair. We can agree to disagree, or we can use our differences as complementary and our similarities as strength to rebuild a foundation, a relationship with respect, with boundaries. There is no reason in this fragile life of ours to maintain a bad feeling or a bad relationship with anyone, whatever they've done. It is worthy to make peace and allow the journey to complete itself peacefully. There's no point holding resentment anymore. Let it go.

Your life is defined by you and no one else but you. You cannot cry for what you create. You have to validate your own journey. Take a step back; look at what you want to build. Instead of blaming and feeling resentful, know that you create whatever you want to.

Let's evolve. Let's move forward and let's start changing the things we want to change to find peace and congruence all around us, with anyone and everyone. Let's become a wholesome unity again.

There's no reason to live with pain. We need joy, love and happiness, knowing that when we reach the end of our days, we've done our best to do everything that was right for everyone around us.

LOOKING AT THE I WITH A DEEPER EYE: MODULE 4

The Context Of My Childhood

Purpose: We look at the stories we grew up with and zoom in to see whether they have influenced the behaviours and stories in our adult lives. Am I repeating any of the patterns that are historical in my family, and is it impacting my life today?

Branch 4.1 – Looking for patterns that I didn't realise were guiding my journey

Goal: I untangle any childhood beliefs that are no longer serving me.

Duality: Appearance vs. reality.

Epiphany: I am not my parents, and I am allowed to make new choices if they serve my children better.

Affirmation: I feel relieved to let go of thoughts and limiting beliefs that no longer have a place in my world.

What we're doing now is zooming in to explore whether stories from our childhood are affecting our adult lives. The question is whether we have unconscious patterns that we are perceiving as being a reality, whereas they may simply be a learnt behaviour.

What was the context of your childhood? Everyone goes through difficult experiences, but they can sometimes be extreme and severe. They can be implicit or explicit.

Was there a physically or mentally abusive parent? Did you have a parent who was unkind or unloving? Did you have an unaffectionate parent? Did you grow up being unaffectionate because you were never cajoled when you were small? Did you have a parent that was mean to your other parent, who beat them up, who was physically abusive? What have you witnessed in your childhood that created the way you are today?

It is not fun to talk about these things, but they are so important to unlock to find resolution and peace. Did you have a parent that took you away and kidnapped you from the other parent, and you never saw your other parent again? Did you have a parent in prison? Did you lose a parent when you were young and were left with memories that were not good? Did you have a parent that you lost when you were young, but you have beautiful memories and find it difficult to live up to the expectations that were upon you? These are topics that challenge all of us, depending on the context of what we experienced when we were children. To define every single one is almost impossible. I urge you to look at your specific situation and then coin the way you work through this module to find your truths to be able to see whether you are punishing yourself by treating yourself badly during your adult life, based upon a childhood map.

Frequently, if we felt unloved, we are overcompensating in our adult lives because we want to feel loved. If you were loved like a princess as a child, you'd be entitled and treat other people badly, perhaps because you think you deserve something that is unfair because you were spoiled. Each one of us has gone through so many different experiences. In our adult lives, our interactions with other people will change based upon the map that we have within, especially in conflictual situations. We tend to revert back to our old patterns unconsciously because of fight or flight. We're in danger. We go back to what we know subconsciously without even realising.

I urge you to take a step back right now, maybe take a deep breath. Close your eyes for a minute and think about what pictures you have in your mind from your childhood that were influencing you and that were difficult. The things that perhaps you are not consciously thinking about anymore, yet you may be reacting badly to without being aware of it.

This is the blueprint to solve any conflict. Appreciating, understanding and measuring our concepts of what we think life and love mean changes everything. You could have had one parent who was abusive, while the other was soft and passive. If as a boy your father was passive while your mother was strong, you may struggle with the male role in your family. If you had a mother who was passive and a father who was a superhero, it will also change the context.

Every situation is unique because each one of us and what we go through is different. Take a step back. Think about it for a minute. Pause if you must. Then we'll move forward.

Were you rebellious or were you calm and quiet? Did you take the trauma and internalise it, or did you externalise it and create a more difficult path for yourself? Often, we're made to feel implicitly that something is our fault without words being exchanged. If nobody ever tells us it's not our fault, how are we to know it?

What is troubling you from your past that you're bringing into your present, and how? If there's nothing, I congratulate you and I celebrate you because most of us carry these little things that we don't even talk about. Sometimes, we don't even share them with our families or any of our loved ones at all. I've had many a client who's come to me and told me stories that they had never told their families or their partners in their adult life. They've held the trauma with them and realise that they're allowed to release it. The child within us believes we're not allowed to release, which is foolish because we end up endangering our families from things that they don't deserve just because we're holding a thought in our minds against ourselves.

I urge you, let's release all of them and empower ourselves to move forward positively without holding any grudges, without holding any trauma from the past, to forgive others, forgive ourselves and be peaceful within. Therefore, we can be peaceful in our external lives, too.

We need to realise that we are not our parents, and we are allowed to make different choices for our futures, for our children. We are allowed to let go of those patterns with awareness to be able to release them positively and permanently. Let's work on this.

Branch 4.2 – Calling a spade 'a spade'

Goal: I identify and release my old patterns to welcome a breath of fresh air.

Duality: Giving in vs. letting go.

Epiphany: Nothing has to be the way I thought it was.

Affirmation: I will behave like the superhero I have always known I am with diligence, dignity and determination.

We are releasing old patterns and triggers to welcome a breath of fresh air and a new way of sensing things. We know that many people copy the patterns of their childhood. We are the only ones who decide what we deserve. We can deserve to use our old patterns to create new behaviours and to actually help our world improve. We can do all kinds of things. What are the voices you're holding subconsciously that we now bring forward to release, forgive, while rewriting the map. Let's move forward with a commitment to ourselves to change those behaviours so that our family, our children, our next generation doesn't suffer for the same things.

Family histories and legacies are so important, and it's only us who are responsible for them. Do we realise that no one else can change our future except for us? How liberating is that? We need await no one else. It's up to us to find the ways to release the past. Start by writing down whatever patterns you have identified. No more blaming anyone for our lives.

We will not inflict our old patterns or wounds upon people we love. If you want to understand the generational patterns, please go back and look at your parents at your age now and see what they were going through. Put yourself in their shoes to try and understand. It helps so much.

'I cried because I had no shoes and then I saw someone who had no feet.'[10] What are we using as our benchmark? Let's change it when we break old patterns.

We walk around with affirmations that suit us. You will find them in *The Muse*. Please use them; repeat them to yourself constantly. It's only by self-affirming, releasing, forgiving and being kind to ourselves that changes happen peacefully and congruently.

We are not victims. We have choices. I know in my life, the biggest freedom was discovering that those choices were mine. It's liberating. The minute we realise we can empower ourselves; everything evolves.

I invite you to welcome your triggers as a friend and teacher. Use them to empower yourself and learn from them, rather than getting angry, flustered and losing your sense of calm. Being angry does not solve anything. If all of us use our triggers as our teachers, we actually have a lot of fun. Watching yourself from a cognitive eye above – like a movie scene with you as director – helps you look at your life, however you choose to perceive it. Celebrate life, release old patterns

---

10   *Good News Network*, 'I cried because I had no shoes, until I met a man who had no feet – Helen Keller' (10 August 2024), www.goodnewsnetwork.org/helen-keller-quote-about-having-no-shoes (accessed October 15, 2024).

and move forward consciously, doing what's right with wisdom, integrity, awareness and a clean eye of what is right and what is wrong. Be accountable, even for the mistakes you make unconsciously. Ignorance is not an excuse for anything.

Even when validating our suffering, we are not allowed to hold on to it. We have to allow it to move on and let it go so that our children don't suffer for it. We have no right to put that onto them. If there are stories of betrayal, infidelity or abuse in your past, do you want to carry them through this fragile life and let them stay with you till the end of it? Is it worth it?

As we know, forgiveness is such an important part of our peace of mind. Even if you don't ever want to speak to that person again, forgive them, forgive yourself. If you can reach out to them and make peace, joy to you, because it actually makes your journey better. It's almost like being selfish to say, 'I want to heal my life. Therefore, I will forgive the other person. I will show an act of selflessness because I want to be selfish and feel good in me.' If that works for you, so be it, but don't leave these things unexplored within you irrespectively. It's not worth it.

We're studying the complexity of yesterday to create the simplicity of tomorrow. It's a journey of pulling out all the worms; it may feel uncomfortable, it may feel troublesome. I thought so for a long, long time, but actually, the minute I started that journey, I realised it was one of peace. It was not as painful as I thought it was going to be. It was a lot easier than I believed.

Faith in me. Faith in you. Faith in us. Faith in unconditional love. Faith in the courage we each possess. Faith that truth eventually emerges. Faith that we can each contribute to make a difference. Faith in our convictions. Faith in divine guidance. Faith in divine justice. Faith in bliss of the afterlife.

Branch 4.3 – Perfecting my prism

Goal: To confirm that the most significant gift I have been afforded is freedom of choice.

Duality: Assertiveness vs. feeling misunderstood.

Epiphany: I determine that my ego is healthy and free of any desire for revenge.

Affirmation: I imagine sandpaper dusting away any remaining fragments of pain from my heart.

The goal here is for us to realise and to confirm that the most substantial gift we've been given in our lives is the freedom of choice. We have a choice to let go of disharmony and embrace harmony. We have a choice to correct the wrongs that we've done in our lives. We have the choice to ask forgiveness and to forgive. That choice is entirely yours. Please embrace that freedom.

Our hearts and minds can be in conflict over how to view a situation, and we can sway from one side to the other. The question is: when the wind blows, are we reaffirmed and feeling freedom or are we scared of the unknown? We tremble when the wind blows. How do you respond to every moment that comes? That choice, too, is yours.

In a difficult situation, you could say, 'Hmm, I wonder why' and embrace it, or you can tremble and be in fear; put the sheets over your head. What good will it do?

How do we strengthen ourselves? How do we grow our vessel to be wholesome, courageous, brave, fulfilled by ourselves, knowing that any big steps we take will celebrate us?

We can be our own heroes and own our stories with pride, or we can remain victims for the rest of our lives. Bad behaviour will never invite good results; if it does, it'll be in the short term until karma kicks in. Find the notion of conscientiousness, benevolence. If you have malevolent intentions, the only person you'll hurt is you. It will neither invite justice nor bring you goodness.

If you are being unfair to your children, to your spouse, to your ex-spouse, you're only going to bring malice to yourself. The point is, by having a benevolent and generous nature, you're able to invite beautiful karma and results into your world. That choice is yours. Do you wish for goodness or harm? If you feel revengeful, who are you helping? If you're trying to hurt other people, what are you doing? Why would you want to bring those results upon yourself? If your ego is telling you, 'I shall win, and they shall lose,' think again. Life is a cycle.

Khalil Gibran has a beautiful saying: 'Do not be delighted because of praise and do not be distressed because of blame […] the trees blossom in spring and bear fruit in summer without seeking praise, and they drop their leaves in autumn and become naked in winter without fearing blame.'[11]

How beautiful. If we know that nature is cyclical, there's always the cycle of life. We know that things can be good one day and terrible the next, and they can be terrible one day and brilliant the next. How do we decide to respond or react if we are trying to control things? We are troubled because we control nothing. You have a choice to decide how you want things to play out; if you want to dance or you want to be rigid. Do you want to cause revenge? To be hurtful to somebody, or to be nice? To be generous, unconditional, loving? You have every choice you want.

The whole notion of what goes around comes around – we know it well. Therefore, we have to choose our battles carefully as to what we want to invite into our

---

11 Khalil Gibran, *The Prophet* (Alfred A. Knopf, 1923)

lives. We have to be able to discern what is important to us and what we can let go of. We require discipline to decide the things that we want to hold to our legacy.

There is so much we can decide, and then we leave the universe to do the rest. A big part of it is a proactive gesture from us. If my ego feels the need to be right rather than do what's right, I will end up lonely. If you prefer to be lonely rather than to find peace and joy, that's not a good choice to make. Knowing I have the freedom to apologise and to find happiness, why would I not choose that path?

Intention is more important than the words a person uses. Setting an intention in any conversation is like drawing a map of where we wish to go – it becomes the driving force behind our goals and aspirations. Without a conscious intention, there is no map, and we are just driving down a road with no destination in mind. People communicate badly sometimes due to certain limitations, misinterpretations, preconditions or premonitions. They nevertheless may hold the best intentions in their hearts.

LOOKING AT THE I WITH A DEEPER EYE: MODULE 5

Regal Responsibilities, Majestic Mindsets And Embracing Empathy

Purpose: We are creating our map towards living with our highest and best philosophies to complement them with practice as an act of elegance, not looking for perfection but enjoying the journey towards joyful living smoothly.

Branch 5.1 – The magic of motherhood

Goal: To know I can create a beautiful journey for my children if I enact exactly as I wish their composure to be.

Duality: Seeking happiness vs. simply being happy.

Epiphany: The sparkle in my child's eye is a result of all the fairy dust I sprinkle on them.

Affirmation: Life can be a light and humorously joyful journey if I so choose it.

We are working on our map towards a wondrous, wholesome journey of self-fulfilment with discipline as an act of elegance. We embrace whatever it is right now and step forward bit by bit to create it magnificently.

I urge you, if you are a father or a child, to look at it from a distance. If you're not a mother, imagine your mother or your spouse and the responsibilities that mothers carry. We can create a beautiful journey for our children if we decide to enact the journey exactly as we would wish it to be for us. We are looking at life from behind their eyes, knowing that we desire to have certain values, graciousness in our world to gift to our children.

You will see your results if you see the sparkle in your child's eye change because of this, or if you imagine what your parents went through if you are the child and see the sparkle you can bring to your own world as a result of your understanding.

Our childhood and the beginning of our amorous relationships define the journey we have as parents. They change the context and shape what we create as a legacy for our child. It's a worthy journey to look forward rather than backward and create a script of how we would want our child's life to play out.

What would you want your child to say about you when they are grown up? Your generosity, your loving, kind nature, your joy, your humour. How are you measuring those aspects from your child's eye? Can you see or remember the things your mother did for you when you were a child? The things that actually touched your heart and tickled you to re-enact them peacefully, joyfully, lovingly?

How far away are you from that role? Are you able to perceive the moments that you found difficult and question whether you're actually imposing those things upon your children? Or whether you are that joyful character that you wish to be? Just as your arrival was an impact and a journey for your mother, so is the same for your children, knowing that it's a child that gives birth to a mother. There is no title of a mother without the child. Who gifted you with your child? Are you appreciative of the way your children came into being? Are you appreciative of the way your parents brought you into being, or do you still hold resentments?

It's time for us to let those go now. The prudence required to create the perfect baseline takes awareness, understanding and tolerance, and it takes discipline, persistence, perseverance and resilience. They say fake it until you make it; fake it until you *become* it.

Create the role that you wish to have and live it day by day; twenty-one days or forty days later, you will be enacting it perfectly.

The challenge of change and all the different roles that we have to play in life open a space to create the superhero out of us. Any gentlemen reading, please celebrate your wives, celebrate your mothers, celebrate the role the woman has to play because, in the olden days, women only had the role of being a mother, a wife. Today, women work, they achieve big careers and they multitask – dramatically multitask – to ensure that all pieces are able to be juggled perfectly.

Women, you need resilience, strength, bravado. If nobody is celebrating you with all the roles you have to play, you have to celebrate yourself. You can't wait for someone else to celebrate you. You have to know that you are amazing at what you're doing. Even if you have to look at yourself in the mirror and tell yourself, 'Every day in every way, I'm getting better and better.'[12] Only we can do that for ourselves; no one does it for us. Don't wait for it from anyone else.

Frequently, men get unhappy when children are born because they lose the attention of their wives. Rather than saying, 'I'm losing her attention', why not say,

---

12 É, Coué, *Self-Mastery Through Conscious Autosuggestion* (American Library Service, 1922)

'Wow, she's doing an amazing job, and I celebrate her, I admire her, I look up to her'?

Many times, people with jealousy will not validate or celebrate you. They will wish to demean you, put you down, act as if you don't exist. How do you respond to that? You don't. You let it be with empathy, knowing that they have their own challenges, their own issues. They can't celebrate you because they feel small. That's OK; they will grow with time. You forgive. You allow it to be what it is. You discern. Don't take anything upon you.

Everyone is struggling in their own journeys. No one is doing something because of you; they're doing it for themselves. Life is actually selfish that way. So long as you accept and realise it, there's no harm in it because it's just the way it is. We can't change that.

Acceptance, harmony, forgiveness, calling a spade 'a spade', as we did in Looking At The I With A Deeper Eye: Module 4, Branch 2, is a notion of letting go, not trying to resist anything. Half our woes are because we want to resist something that we think someone else is making us feel. Why don't we just accept it?

People are all different. People have characters, and it's OK. They will be who they are, and we can be who we are. So long as we step up, lift up and decide to embrace whatever comes along our paths.

Why resist it? What good will it do when children are born to couples? The disinterest rather than devotion of the mother towards the father is something to be careful of because that's usually the time when couples have issues. The important thing to realise is that women have other responsibilities. They go through physical changes in their bodies. Men have to be empathetic towards that, rather than running off and doing silly things.

We have to realise that there's a balance to be struck between the roles that we all play. That's OK; it just requires a little attentiveness. If I don't know how to ask for what I need, how can I be sure to get it? I have to be able to communicate my desires in a way that they are received beautifully, not as nagging or as a demand. I have to be able to create empathy in the other person to ask for what I need and say how I'm feeling.

Many times, we think vulnerability is terrible in these cases. It's not; it helps build bridges and the relationship gets closer and stronger. Remember that our children absorb us fully, wholesomely. Even if they don't say things explicitly, you know that one day, whatever we create will come back to us. Breathe things carefully, gently and lovingly.

Branch 5.2 – Releasing the riot of resentment

Goal: To centre my truth that is uniquely mine.

Duality: Risk vs. reward.

Epiphany: No one makes me feel anything without my permission.

Affirmation: I will witness my thoughts carefully to untangle any limiting beliefs.

This is about centring our truths that are uniquely ours. As we know from Enter the Garden, Eleanor Roosevelt said, 'No one makes you feel anything without your permission.'[13] What if I unconsciously accepted truths that were, in fact, coming from outside that don't belong to me? They're not mine because they don't suit me. It's somebody else's impression. Can you think of an example of something that you've taken as being a truth for you, which actually has no resonance with you?

Real learning involves unlearning all the patterns. All the noises. All the teachers. All the figureheads that we respected, or things people said about us. Is there a good reason to hold on to them still or would you prefer to let them go? Would you prefer to be dancing the lambada on a beachside or sitting locked up in

---

13   E Roosevelt, *This Is My Story* (Harper & Brothers, 1937)

your bedroom with the windows closed and locked? It's your choice.

You will do whichever you decide, but know what is best for you, for those you love and for those who love you. Excessive praise from the outside world or its opposite, the blame, are both not useful to decipher who we are. We can let go of any praise, let go of any blame and just be constant with ourselves. We know that the only person whose approval we need is our own, so long as we are living to our highest and best standards. Whatever anyone else thinks is from their mindset, not about us. You are creating, in fact, whatever you decide. What a freedom, what a beauty! Do you still want to hold on to the riot of resentment?

We must be cautious of the words 'betrayal' or 'boredom'. Both can betray us ourselves. We say, 'we are boring if we say we are bored'; it means we're not creating a life for ourselves. If we feel betrayed, have we betrayed someone to feel betrayed? Or are we saying betrayal is ours from them, but not identifying that we may have betrayed them first by being cruel, unkind, ungenerous or unloving?

What does the word 'acceptance' mean to you? Do you feel you are never accepted or do you feel you never accepted someone in your life?

What does the word 'approval' mean to you? Do you actually disapprove of people and show them with the expressions on your face? Are you mirroring something that was a disapproving look you had from your family?

You need to be conscientious of every step of this journey to know what you're creating. It's in micro expressions. Your micro expression speaks just as your energy speaks. You have to align from your physical behaviour to your micro expressions to your energy within. All that stems from the baseline of you and all the images and experiences you're holding – if you're holding them still, you need to let them go or identify and reframe them to what you wish them to be.

What does the word 'retrospect' mean to you today? What have you seen as changes or messages that you're identifying that we've gone through so far?

What does 'tolerance' mean? Can we up our game of tolerance to open ourselves and be a little more understanding, empathetic and joyful in receiving that we could not receive before, because our eye was too geared towards ourselves rather than outward-looking to see how other people are feeling? Are you able to turn your eye around now and see how life is from behind the other person's eye, whoever that may be: your child, your parent, your partner? It can be anybody.

We all have the ability to look at life not from behind our eyes anymore, but from behind the other person's eyes to reframe things carefully, diligently, responsibly, with dignity. We can do that. We have a responsibility to do that. It's not always me, me, me, me, me. It has to be that you turn your eye away from you now, look at the other and see how they are feeling.

What have I created in their journey? Have I brought blessings to them, or have I been a misery? When did you feel belittled? When did you feel self-absorbed? When did you feel as though you weren't good enough? Do you feel fearful to confront someone? Are you scared of their reply? Can you change your tonality to be welcoming, kind and assertive? It changes their responses and the results.

If our ego is hurt or shattered, we will be scared to say something because we're scared to be hurt again. If we change our reply, we change the way we say something, and we even humour ourselves. You say, 'Well, I was foolish, and I'm so sorry.' You don't have to stay proud. You can be humble and say, 'You know what? I was an idiot. I'm so sorry. I made a mistake. Please forgive me. Allow me to make it up to you. I can do better now. I can be a nicer person. I can change. I can learn. I can heal. I am healing. I am healed.' All of these things are possible.

Much of the time, we are on the defensive because we don't want to open our hearts, out of fear of being hurt. We play it cool, or we push back so we don't get hurt. Actually, that's pure vulnerability, which is disguised in fear, in detachment, in coldness because we're scared. Can you admit that you were scared to feel hurt? Can you admit that you were scared to have your heart touched, tickled or cajoled and it created more fear in you rather than joy? Many of us find it hard to feel happy. A lot of us have a fear of happiness because once we achieve that happiness, we're scared of losing it.

If we don't give it a chance, do we prefer to stay in misery, feeling unloved? Why? It's better to take the risk and feel rewarded as a result. It's a beautiful life we have, and we complicate it so much, so unnecessarily, all because we don't want to peel off the layers and lay ourselves bare. The best gift you can give yourself is to allow yourself to be vulnerable, to be bare, to be open, to allow your heart to be open, to feel anything you need to feel and experience it. As a result, grow, develop and celebrate your person.

The key to authenticity is to be able to stand in front of the mirror, admit your truths to yourself and then celebrate yourself openly. It starts with you, then you can move on to the other person that you want to heal with. Stand in front of the mirror and look at yourself carefully, celebrate yourself, be kind to yourself, forgive yourself and be willing to now turn the chapter. Change the page and move forward to a life that you're creating of joy, happiness, abundance and a no-more-poverty mentality.

It's all about generosity and abundance. You release the pain, you let it go, and you vow to yourself that you will not make the same mistakes going forward. You will allow your children and your future partner, future children, to grow into being the most beautiful human beings they can be. They will celebrate you, and you will celebrate them. Together, all this is possible.

Branch 5.3 – Roles and responsibilities

Goal: Seeing life from behind my children's eyes, I know I can create harmony, structure and balance for them, irrespective of circumstances that surround me.

Duality: Disconnection and disbelief vs. commitment and conviction.

Epiphany: My children do not have to be burdened with anything they do not deserve to endure.

Affirmation: Everything can be simple and easy, depending on the path I pave for myself and my loved ones from here on.

I know I can create structure, harmony and joy, irrespective of the circumstances that surround me. I'm able to create whatever I decide to create from here on – what a joy! Everything can be simple, depending on the path I choose to pave for myself, knowing it is only my responsibility, my accountability and no one else's. What a freedom!

If you are young and you don't have children yet, the way to perceive this content is from behind the eyes of your parents when you were a child and how you see your role today in going forward or in your relationship with your parents now, should it be difficult.

We all have a choice in what we create, and we can all undo any wrongs. We can untangle any misconceptions, misunderstandings, misdemeanours. We all have the capacity to do so.

What does trust mean to me in these circumstances? How am I portraying my trust? How are my children perceiving trust? How do my parents perceive trust? What is my relationship with trust? Trust in me. Trust in you. Trust in the universe.

Are we hopeful and optimistic, or do we want to be begrudging, complaining and unkind? Does it help? What does it help? What boundaries are we practising? Are we being selfish and unkind by showing our children our dismay of life? Are we putting upon them issues that they don't need to face, just because we are selfish and we're thinking only of ourselves, or are we being kind and protecting them, cushioning them with cosiness irrespective of how we're feeling?

Are there things that you or your parent complained about that hurt you deeply and had nothing to do with you? Can you forgive it and let it go now?

Am I forcing my children to adopt my map of how life is difficult, unkind and unfair or am I allowing them to have the best of intentions to rock the world and be happy and joyful to create and be creative? What am I doing? What am I creating based upon who I am today? Am I sharing with my children my fear of the unknown or am I preparing them carefully?

Being the gatekeeper to show them the path of the world ahead, protecting them, knowing that they're capable with the courage of achieving anything they wish. What is my responsibility to feed into my child's DNA in terms of what life looks like? What is the map of responsibility? Creating their responsibility, their sense of responsibility for their life and to protect us too?

A child needs all the values in the world. Did you create them for your children? Did your parents create them for you, or are you aware of things that you wish to adopt today for your tomorrow? Because you can do that now peacefully and wholesomely. The irony is that if we're not acting out of our integrity, we beat ourselves up. If we've made it a cycle to beat ourselves up constantly because we are not practising our highest integrity, then what can we expect to create?

Let's change all those patterns now. Let's reframe them one by one. Write all the things down that you wish to reframe. Write the change that you wish to make and – every day in every way – practise it until it becomes your habit, knowing that anything is possible. I assure you; I say it from my heart because I did it myself.

We can all continue this journey peacefully and happily with integrity and passion. We can all create joy and purpose in our lives, irrespective of the circumstances that we've had or that we have now. We can change them. Please know it, understand it, breathe it. We can change anything. Allow for food for thought and perspective.

Don't impose your opinions upon others. Let them have their own opinions. Validate them. Share their excitement and joy, and know, you too can be part of that joy. Because if you decide to stay in misery and they are joyful, and they're moving forward and you are being selfish, what are you going to achieve? You are going to lose them, and there is no need for that.

Welcome anyone for where they are in their journey and celebrate them with hope, joy, possibility of what they can achieve. Ask them for forgiveness to let things go and tell them that you're sorry, and that you were unkind because you didn't realise any better. Can you do that? Will you? It doesn't mean we need to manipulate anyone. We're allowed to be true. We can admit our mistakes. We can admit that we are angry and resentful. We can say that we've understood things better now, and we're willing to let them go.

It is such an important thing to do, I assure you. Don't be selfish and force people to fulfil your map of how you want life to play out. It's not fair. Give them the freedom to create the lives that they want without any push or pull. Putting down the rope, not holding it to tug on it. Allow others to be free so that you can be free too. We all have to be accountable for an integral life without ego, without selfishness. Wishing the best for all our loved ones, for all that we encounter, for anyone that we have a deal with.

Being unkind is a waste of time and is extremely selfish and egotistical. Imagine that everyone changed their tune to become more generous in wanting others to feel good, what would our world look like? How would it change? How beautiful can it be? Even if we don't want to, let's do it with discernment. Let's do it because it will help our loved ones and anyone we encounter along our paths, and bring us back the good karma as well.

LOOKING AT THE I WITH A DEEPER EYE: MODULE 6

Meditation And Mediation

Purpose: Our children do not belong to us; they are our keepsakes. We have no right to impose anything on them but rather be an exemplary gatekeeper, holding their space with only their best interest in mind and heart.

Branch 6.1 – Nullifying the negative narrative

Goal: From a higher dimension, I now know that I must be fair to my offspring, or else it is only I who will lose out in the future.

Duality: Validate my truth vs. falsify to fit in.

Epiphany: I release my ego and allow compassion and the benefit of the doubt to engage in meaningful dialogue to improve our collective journey.

Affirmation: I am able to find reasons why things happened the way they did with forgiveness and self-awareness to create a dignified destiny.

The module heading, Meditation and Mediation, means that we find the space within ourselves to now open up, change our perspectives and mediate to good results. To change any disharmony that we've had into collaboration and collectively find a conscientious journey to achieve good results.

The branch heading, Nullifying the Negative Narrative, is apt because holding the resentments, holding any grudges, holding any pain deep within doesn't result in proper outcomes. It requires us to step out of this to actually nullify it so that we may move forward peacefully and positively. We do not want to keep any residue.

Holding any threads or fragments of pain allows for nothing. With the pain released, what are the ways, perspectives and things that you will now look at to change the outcomes? Once the dust has settled, what can you see differently now that you've removed a negative perspective from your mind? How can you reframe the words and feelings?

I release my ego, and I allow compassion. I welcome compassion. I allow the benefit of the doubt to establish that I perhaps was not right in all of my thoughts, all of my reactions, all of my anticipations of what the other person was doing to now find new results, new perspectives. It's freeing, and it feels great. I am now able to find the reasons why things perhaps happened differently to how I thought, and I'm able to create a dignified destiny of peace and harmony, of togetherness.

When the mind finds calm, we can see that situations are not as hopeless as we may have anticipated. Bridges can be mended. Things can evolve. People can come together harmoniously again. How many times have I witnessed families that were disrupted that come together and find a beautiful path together. It doesn't have to be hopeless, and it's no longer hopeless because you can see, as I can, that everything can change for the better, for everyone's better. You can discern and deliberate your responses to old behaviours.

You can reframe your previous reactions and surprise people with the new you. They will welcome it graciously. Have no fear. When we observe ourselves with calm detachment, we can open up so many realms of possibility.

What choices do you want to make today, now that you're seeing things from a different eye? There is no purpose to stay in tunnel vision anymore. Let's open some windows, see things from a different eye and invite new responses.

What are the first things you're going to do? Write them down so that you don't lose them. As we have pondered, where do thoughts come from, and where do they go? It's so important to hold on to them when you have an epiphany – when you have an 'aha' moment – so that you can actually breed those changes that you wish to start establishing. We can witness that we were poised between two different realities before, in the dualities.

Depending on which eye you give something, everything can change. Are you willing now to make those changes? Are you ready? Our sense of urgency and emergency stemmed from within. The minute we find that calm, we know that there is more urgency and we can take a step back, breathe peacefully and calmly, and open up a realm of possibility of everything new.

We're allowed to surrender to the cards that life plays out with our new beginnings. We're allowed to have the courage to make changes. The minute we invite graceful behaviour, synchronicity enters our lives. The minute we become aware of synchronicity – where things happen magically and naturally – we lift our vibration to witness something so beautiful. I invite you to join me on that journey.

The power is within us to release all the disharmony now and to open up this pathway. Being and becoming, stretching ourselves, opening it up, allowing abnormal circumstances to invite new beginnings. You know, we are all made up of two individuals, a father and a mother. All of us carry history and ancestry that stems from many different people. Our responsibility today is to open up the pathway to create harmony all around us, irrespective of any shadows or fragments of pain that were from our past. We have to be willing to do so and nullify the negative narrative.

Branch 6.2 – Disclosure with disclaimer

Goal: To understand the journey towards resolution is with the realisation that we are all responsible.

Duality: Selfishness vs. selflessness.

Epiphany: Vulnerability is an absolute strength.

Affirmation: What I imagined was worse than the reality. I can change my impressions and find a change of perspective, and I can breathe a sigh of relief.

I love the heading Disclosure with Disclaimer because it says that we are willing now to disclose all the epiphanies we've had, with a disclaimer that we didn't know that we didn't know these things before. No one can turn around today and blame you again for things you did in the past; on the contrary, they should welcome your response.

Why disclosure? Because becoming naked to some truths that we need to bear, that we need to share, is not an easy journey. It's a worthy one, but it doesn't mean that it's simple.

Let's take the steps towards it. What does it require? It requires you to be vulnerable in front of yourself, to be vulnerable in front of the other person. If you need to disclose realities of yours that were not shared, how would you do that? Would you say, 'I was wrong' or would you say, 'This was my impression at that time and I'm sorry I misunderstood you'?

The way you speak and the words you choose make a big difference as to the outcome. You must be careful not to say, 'You were wrong.' You should say, 'I perceived the situation as wrong. Today, I can see it from a different eye.' We're maintaining boundaries, and we're allowing reality to be what it is. It doesn't mean that you have to fall to the ground to beg someone.

No, in humility, you're able to admit your faults without putting any blame or negative charge on the other person. You're taking the disclaimer, 'Hey, I didn't know that I didn't know. I didn't know that I wasn't respectful until I was. I didn't know that I wasn't understanding until I was.' Once you've journeyed towards congruences there's no going back because your third eye is open now and you're able to perceive things differently.

Going forward, please don't believe that you're lowering yourself by admitting something to somebody else. It's quite the contrary. You're actually raising yourself higher because you're taking a different stance in dignity, in humility, with integrity to say, 'Yes, I may have been wrong and that's OK because today I am here to make amends and make things better.'

I don't want my children to suffer. I don't want my parents to suffer. I don't want my spouse to suffer. I don't want my ex-spouse to suffer. I don't want my colleagues to suffer. I want to be integral, and I want to do what is right for everyone. I'm willing to find the balance, to find the pieces to put together to make it peaceful. If I had a false ego and I was selfish, I am sorry. It's not that hard to say it if you are willing. Am I able to be the bigger person?

If you don't want to say you are wrong, are you willing to share in the responsibility where you can find some sort of compromise and say, 'Well, I misunderstood this, and you misunderstood that'? Are you able to say, 'I take my share of responsibility. Please take yours so that it can be solved and end this horrible situation, whatever it may be'?

A lot of times, we don't think we have possibilities or solutions. There's a realm of possibility. There's a million solutions. It's just about finding the right one that works for you and that you're comfortable with. The minute you're congruent, everything else will fall into place. Let's be generous in our assumptions.

Let's assume, because right now you're probably thinking, 'The other person's not going to react well. They're not going to say the right thing.' If we're generous in our assumptions, the other person is probably going to be stunned. They're probably not going to respond immediately. They will mull it over and they won't know how to react because they're not used to you speaking like this.

Let's say we give them that generous assumption, and we leave them room. We don't anticipate that they're going to respond immediately and get upset if they don't. No; we allow them time. We give them time and we sit with the discomfort, being comfortable with the discomfort of waiting for them to find that sense of peace and for us to put all the energy to the universe to make it happen graciously. It makes all the difference, because if we're anticipating a negative response it's probably already lost.

You need to be in a space where even if the other person is going to respond negatively, you're willing and able because you know that you're doing what is right. You know you're doing things from your highest and best. Whatever response you receive will be OK because you have said what you needed to say.

Your accountability and responsibility is yours. The other person's response is not actually part of your intention. Your intention is to do what is right for everyone involved. Therefore, the best thing you can do is to open yourself and say, 'I am willing to do this for the right reasons, for the right responses, and I am willing to anticipate that I can receive the right response.'

Remember that the person in question was once important to you and someone you were communicating well with. Therefore, there's no reason why you can't find good communication again. If it's a parent–child relationship, you know that the seeds of love are already planted. Therefore, watering them and bringing them back to life is not difficult. On the contrary, it's beautiful.

I am vulnerable, and I am allowing myself to disclose my truths with the disclaimer that I will protect myself if I need to, yet, with the knowledge that I have done what's right and I've done everything to the best of my ability.

Branch 6.3 – The roller coaster towards repair and restoration

Goal: To learn to dance again from a different platform, knowing that with time and practice, it can be any dance I wish. Distant shadows turn into a sunny flow, and I learn to dance in the breeze.

Duality: Discretion vs. subtlety.

Epiphany: As bittersweet as it is, I know I am doing this for the joy of my children.

Affirmation: My family is healing, and I am giving my children the best choice of balanced joy in their lives.

We learn to dance again from a different perspective, feeling a fresh breeze, removing any shadows from the past and dancing joyfully in the sunlight again.

The distant shadows have become a sunny flow. How does it feel? As bittersweet as it is, it's a joyful experience, as vulnerable as we're feeling and as hard as it may feel. It's a worthy journey. I encourage you to take all the steps necessary to find this peace and bliss in proximity with detachment.

Accepting people as they are, for who they are, no longer projecting your expectations upon them. Willing to see them openly for who they are and happy for them to be who they are without forcing anything – forgiving the hurt and moving past it. If you want to keep the memories of pain, they're just going to regurgitate again. Let them go.

Trust in yourself. Trust in your ability to respond appropriately. Give each person the chance to redeem themselves without you wanting to remind them of any pain. There's no longer any need to punish anyone because you're peaceful and calm within. You're no longer holding on to it, so no one else has to. Remember that you once shared the love too.

Even siblings who have fallen out can find a place where they used to play together and get that relationship back – harvesting it naturally, healthily in the right way – purification of the senses and purification of the will. Purifying the senses is releasing them from the tyranny of judgement. Seeing something as if it's a fresh canvas. Imagine a painting. You've already painted it, you've seen it, you've been looking at it for so many years. Now it's time to look at it from a completely new angle. See the person with whom you're going to interact as a blank canvas. You're just open, listening, observing and witnessing them for who they are, now.

You can do a measurement of who they were versus who they are later – no need to do that in your first interaction. The first thing is opening the gate to healing, allowing someone else to be in your space that you've had difficulty with, being able to sit in that same space, peacefully and openly.

We crash our selfish interpretations and we open ourselves to seeing things as a new reality. Not against us, but for us. Because in that moment, exactly what happens is from the inside of our deeper eye. We look at it and say, 'Oh dear, what's going on here?' We feel threatened. It's a natural reaction – one we can anticipate.

The key is to tell yourself in that moment that it's all going to be fine because you have the highest and best in mind. There's no need to let that vulnerability be a bad thing. On the contrary, take it on. Wear it as an armour of strength because you're being completely honest and open – no longer wearing any masks. Be willing to admit your faults, willing to admit your humility and say, 'I want this situation to be better because I know that you meant something to me before. I don't want to lose you in my world in whichever possible way, even if it's just to make peace and move on.'

Self-simplification is the key – no need to complicate matters anymore. Let's get it down to basics, that actually allows it to be easier for all of us – step one, step two, step three. No need to overcomplicate the mind. No need to anticipate reactions. Just be and breathe.

Purity is an affirmative state. Clear, pure, strong. It allows you to hold yourself in a position of dignity. No need to wait for a negative response. No need to anticipate anything, just be. All prejudice removed. No need for blame anymore. Wow! How does that feel?

Yes, it can feel uncomfortable in the heart. Yes, it can feel nerve-racking and you can have a tremble. You're seeing things with new eyes. You're releasing your old anguishes and negative patterns – everything's gone. Yes, the body has memories of pain; if you're fully in your awareness, you may feel little things here or there in your body, and that's OK, too. You can forgive it and say, 'You know what, don't worry. It's OK.'

Reaching a place of sensation with an open heart, with no thoughts, it's a beautiful feeling. Keats perceived a life of sensation without thought to be the key to pure happiness.[14] We have often judged ourselves to be right or wrong, depending on what we're perceiving. What a liberation to let go of thinking and just feel. We let go of the past; we have forgiven it. The next step in the right direction is to open up a bridge of beautiful communication, even if it's just for the sake of children, parents or a spouse or ex-spouse.

With your generous heart, absolutely anything is possible when your heart is in flow. There is no awaiting love. It is inconsequential because you are full of love.

---

14 J Keats, *Letters of John Keats* (Rollins, H. E., ed., Harvard University Press, 1958) [First written in a letter to Benjamin Bailey, 22 November 1817], www.azquotes.com/quote/377253

THE HUMAN TOUCH

The possibilities of the universe are far richer and simpler than we imagined. By becoming calm, peaceful and wholesome, every step of the way becomes easy. There's no overthinking anymore. It's time to let go. Bridge all those gaps. It's time to make amends of things from the past so that our futures may be wholesome, complete, joyful and happy.

I hope that Looking At The I With A Deeper Eye has been helpful to you in resolving any conflicts. Please don't hesitate to reach out if I may be of assistance to enhance the perfect harmony in your world.

✉ humantouch@gardenofayden.com

Conclusion

The guiding principles of *The Human Touch*

May the guiding principles of *The Human Touch* assist you to carve and nurture your journey with grace and splendour. We also invite you to download *The Muse*, your companion to safeguard your contemplations.

The Anchor: May we be grounded, with feet well anchored in the earth and engrained with a vivid spirit.

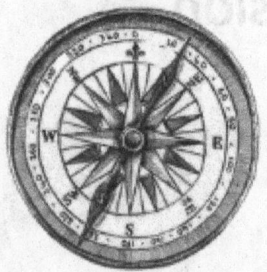

The Compass: May we be guided in the right direction and have our moral compasses intact.

The Globe: May we feel capable to conquer the world with knowledge, may we protect the earth and may we be socially responsible.

The Orange tree: May we stop to smell the blossoms and may all that we work on bear fruit.

CONCLUSION

The Muse – Stepping from contemplation into action

You are invited to complete *The Muse* online or download it to use as your workbook to embed all the thoughts, wishes and commitments you are making to yourself for the journey ahead.

www.gardenofayden.com/the-muse

Emptiness is only felt when we seek solace in the wrong place. It may nag us until we awaken to our truths, which fill us deeply. The journey is about unlearning and the end of sabotage.

- We maintain a positive self-belief with no negative associations.

- We allow no unease to enter our minds to ensure no disease in our bodies.

- We iron out all misunderstandings and misperceptions.

- We accept the truths and realities of others, without letting our past punish our present.

- We get comfortable with discomfort, knowing that letting go does not mean we agree.

- We know that validating others allows them to feel heard, while we are always careful not to impose our truths.

- We maintain respectful boundaries.

It is our inner make up that creates our outer refinement. We gift ourselves with the opportunity to plant and harvest the seeds of our souls within. We ignite our inner sparkle to share it in our outer world, where we may all speak the same language and can seamlessly understand each other, with no room for ego, misunderstanding, or fear to offend.

We may truly breathe in the notion of 'our secret garden' to live our internal world colourfully, with our most creative imagination. This in turn spills over into our external world. The sparkle of our eyes, the energy we exuberate, the way we express ourselves and how people then respond to us. We will have somewhat silenced our minds based upon a deep resonance within our souls where we understand ourselves and hence understand others better.

Altruism is defined as a disinterested and selfless concern for the well-being of others, knowing that we are all connecting under the same stars, touching the same sea. We have witnessed such a beautiful globally united front of togetherness to stand with humanity. Let's continue to tie the thread of unity collectively as we know that our efforts need to be towards a love for humaneness and tolerance towards all.

Garden of Ayden is a twist on Garden of Eden, a modern-day utopia. Ayden means non-judgement, non-attachment, non-resistance.

May your garden always nourish you deeply.

Wishing you beauty, bliss and blessings and sending you and your loved ones my best wishes for a deeply fulfilling life.

Meditation

Last, but absolutely not least, here are two valuable resources. The first is your daily companion to truly shift the inner workings of your being as you engage with your daily rituals. It's only eight minutes and it is an inspiring meditation to bring you truly to your highest and best.

www.gardenofayden.com/meditation

The second is our Garden of Ayden Radio Playlist to enhance the contemplation and even perhaps to enjoy while reading.

https://open.spotify.com/playlist/7IJtzTKeIx
QHszteuXPVm1?si=1G9A2mawRC2Od3G
z1lf3dg

Epilogue

Reflective and thought-provoking.

Vulnerable and genuine.

Authentic, sharp and powerful.

Those seeds of wisdom are forever ours to keep.

I was deeply moved by the journey we undertook as we moved through different stages: from understanding these seeds to integrating them and, ultimately, allowing them to flourish.

May they forever keep on blooming within us and may our garden inspire others to plant their seeds too, benefiting generations to come.

I love this journey of the soul that we are on and in this book, Suki helps us understand how we are all in this together and how we are never alone in our quest, trials, errors and triumphs.

This work stands as a powerful testament of love, truth and compassion, reminding us that regardless of our backgrounds, we are all students of life, united in the pursuit of becoming our best selves.

With its refreshing perspective and unique methodology, this book offers a clear and engaging outlook on life. I highly recommend it to all soul-seekers, whether seasoned travellers or beginners on their inner journey.

May this book illuminate our blind spots and light our way forward.

Laura Bounin, Founder of AuraMembers Club, from Paris, France, living in London, UK

Celebrating *The Human TOUCH*

'The market abounds with personal development books, yet *The Human TOUCH* stands out, anchored in the author's profound experience and pragmatic wisdom. While verbose theories rarely appeal to me, I found its original insights and practical, pertinent guidance invaluable for fostering meaningful self-reflection'.

— **Philippe Gudin**, Switzerland

'Enjoy a sharp and accurate insight into human behaviour in this superb book. Sukaiyna's words are warm, encouraging, and relatable. Her anecdotes and conversational tone create an infallible connection with all readers regardless of gender, creed, and geo location.

'Revel in this promising and valuable resource while permeating your soul with the scent of the roses in the Garden of Ayden!'
— **Mary-Louise Hagerty**, in Residence in Asuncion, Paraguay

'With heartfelt wisdom and profound insight, Garden of Ayden invites readers to embark on a journey of self-reflection and transformation. Sukaiyna masterfully weaves personal experiences with universal values, creating a practical guide to unlocking the hidden gems within ourselves. A deeply inspiring resource for cultivating peace, purpose and authenticity.'
— **Annika Pergament**, United States of America

'*The Human TOUCH* by Sukaiyna Gokal offers a compelling and practical roadmap to uncover patterns and mitigate triggers, fostering awareness and embracing forgiveness. This insightful guide empowers readers to nullify negative narratives and embrace accountability on their journey toward emotional growth.'
— **Piero Incisa della Rochetta**, from Italy living in Spain and Patagonia

'*The Human TOUCH* is an inspiring guide to self-growth. Sukaiyna shares simple tools and heartfelt wisdom to help readers heal, connect and find harmony in life.'
— **Dina Shirazi**, Bahrain

'*The Human TOUCH* takes you on a journey to find inner serenity: Sukaiyna's work combines a guide to navigate your inner self, a toolkit for re-assessing and embracing your reality, a recipe book for creating a new perspective and a formula for achieving liberation through the balance of a new mindset... very enlightening, to say the least.'
   — **Ahmad Shaker**, Switzerland

'A powerful message delivered in a most elegant manner, through a delight of a read! This book speaks to the heart, helping one to see the world and this mysterious life through the lens of acceptance and compassion.'
   — **Yustina Filat**, from Republic of Moldova, living in Bali, Indonesia

'*The Human TOUCH* is a piece of art that deeply describes the concept of life. It gifts us with a mirror of strength, patience, integrity, hard work and love, to nurture effortlessly in our daily lives. *Pour vivre heureux, vivons cachés.*'
   — **Emmanuel J. Bally**, Switzerland and United Arab Emirates

'*The Human TOUCH* by Sukaiyna Gokal is a transformative guide to self-reflection and personal growth. With profound insights and practical tools, Sukaiyna offers readers a compassionate roadmap to untangle limiting beliefs, cultivate self-awareness and embrace our shared humanity. This book is a gentle yet powerful invitation to polish the mirror of our souls and unlock our highest potential.'

— **Nailesh Khimji**, Oman

'When you send your ego on holiday and embrace your inner Director, as Sukaiyna beautifully guides, the transformative power of TOUCH awakens within – Tolerance dissolves judgment, Openness welcomes growth, Unity connects hearts, Collaboration sparks creativity and Harmony orchestrates life's symphony into a masterpiece of purposeful achievement and authentic connection.'

— **Cyrus Hodes**, from France, living in the United States of America, United Arab Emirates and Singapore

'*The Human TOUCH* by Sukaiyna Gokal is an honest exploration that guides towards enlightening epiphanies that lead to inner peace and to building meaningful connections. With practical affirmations and gentle encouragement, it inspires love, joy and compassion. A timeless guide I'll keep close by to revisit often for its wisdom and comfort. A must-read.'

— **Alejandra Frade Rotlander**, Madrid, Spain

'We all need a good spiritual guide or mentor to show us the way in the deepest corners of our heart and soul. Entering our Garden of Eden and finding the proper exit into purposeful ways is what this journey is all about. For whichever outcome you choose, this book will be the light that guides you through it'

— **Omar Danial**, Switzerland

'Reading this book felt like uncovering a part of myself I didn't know was there. It showed me how something as simple as human touch can reveal my true feelings and help me understand who I really am. This isn't just a book—it's a companion and a toolkit that guided me to embrace my authentic self and act with confidence.'

— **Philippe Tourbier**, from France, living in Dubai

'Sukaiyna Gokal's *The Human TOUCH* is a profound guide to self-discovery, offering tools to untangle inherited narratives and uncover inner truth. With practical methods, it empowers readers to achieve peace, harmony and fulfilment. A lifelong companion, it deepens self-awareness and growth with every reread, inspiring alignment with one's best self.'

— **Lara Sabella**, Amman Jordan

'*The Human TOUCH* challenges our perception of self, life and to work through personal pain or tragedy. Realising the limitations of our egos, we relinquish clinging to anger and the past. This results in suffering less from negativity and moving towards freedom in life, releasing the blinding shortcomings of the past into the light.'

— **Joe Lau**, from China, living in Hong Kong

'*The Human TOUCH* by Sukaiyna Gokal is an ingenious guide to self-discovery, empathy and personal growth. With reflective tools and profound insights, it empowers readers to embrace forgiveness, foster inner peace and nurture meaningful relationships. Truly life-changing!'

 — **Alison Tabiaat**, from South Africa, living in Oman

'This profound guide taught me that liberation comes from releasing old narratives. I learned to treat triggers as teachers, breathe through difficulties like air through valves and view life through a "director's lens". Most transformatively, I discovered that love flows naturally when we stop seeking validation and start practicing unconditional acceptance.'

 — **Nejm Serraoui**, from Algeria, living in London, United Kingdom and Dubai, United Arab Emirates

'Sukaiyna Gokal has undertaken an incredibly ambitious project; bringing together a comprehensive guide for a complete personal reset. It covers every aspect of exploration and self-discovery. Easy to understand, well-written and laid out in a readily digestible format. With examples and memorable epithets, it will help even the most cynical reader find invaluable comfort and wisdom.'

 — **Katinka Gissing**, London, United Kingdom

I very much enjoyed reading Sukaiyna Gokal's first book, "The Human Touch". The entire reading experience was like a journey with her reflective and thoughtful writing. The interactive challenges were both thought provoking and enlightening. As you read her book, let your heart open and embrace the profound knowledge Sukaiyna shares from "The Garden of Ayden." It's amazing!
— **Stuart Barton**, United States of America

'Empowering, insightful and transformative. *The Human TOUCH* is a guiding light for anyone seeking to unlock their potential and embrace the best version of themselves.'
— **Rawan Sirry**, Dubai, United Arab Emirates

'*The Human TOUCH* blends empathy with insight, offering a heartfelt guide to self-healing and connection. Having worked closely with Suki, I've seen her genuine care for growth and understanding. This book is a heartfelt companion for anyone seeking clarity, deeper relationships and the strength to understanding the art of being human.'
— **Muhammad Bilal**, from Pakistan, living in Georgia

'*The Human TOUCH* arrived at a pivotal moment in my life, providing profound insights into self-awareness. As I navigate this turning point, its teachings on empathy, introspection and connection resonate deeply, guiding me toward meaningful change and a renewed sense of purpose.'

— **Jacques Bounin**, Paris, France

'*The Human TOUCH* delivers a powerhouse of distilled wisdom, drawing from a rich tapestry of personal experience, research and timeless philosophies. A powerful step-by-step guide, no matter where you are on your journey, to achieve a more fulfilled and compassionate life. In essence, a calling to let go and lead with love.'

— **Leila Azmoudeh**, London, United Kingdom

'*The Human TOUCH* creates a transformative pathway that encourages readers to embrace endless possibilities through shedding ego and surrendering to their inner light. This healing and human connection guide teaches unconditional giving, love and empathy, thus allowing one's heart and mind to embrace lifelong fulfilment, true enrichment, and meaningful relationships.'

— **J. Scott Stover**, United States of America

'A must-read – *The Human TOUCH* by Sukaiyna Gokal. The book guides readers through self-discovery and growth, emphasising authenticity, fulfilment and inner peace. The book inspires prioritising inner happiness, conquering challenges and living purposefully. Sukaiyna's words offer guidance, encouraging readers to embrace their

true selves, navigate life with resilience and unlock their potential.'
— **Farnaz Fazaipour**, London,
   United Kingdom

'In *The Human TOUCH*, Ms Sukaiyna Gokal offers a poignant exploration of self-discovery and healing. Her unique perspective illuminates the transformative power of empathy and connection, urging us to embrace tolerance and unity. A heartfelt guide that inspires readers to cultivate their inner gardens with grace.'
— **Samar Jodha**, from India, living
   in New Delhi

'This handbook for personal esteem provides a masterly insight to the values, concepts and prejudices that we may have carried from childhood. Carefully guided, we are set up to redevelop and enhance our relationships with those around us and thereby find a degree of happiness and self-perception to envigorate our own lives. Bravo!'
— **Lucia Hofbauer**, from Germany, living
   in Switzerland

'Bless Sukaiyna Gokal… for her brave and thoughtful work, a collection of ideas arising from her intelligence and heart, grown from the wisdom of life.

'As a parent I feel her words profoundly and I'm grateful for her affecting change in global society by imparting caring approaches to our primordial challenges.

'Through communication we evolve.'
— **Mr. Chantaka 'Jay' Puranananda**, from Thailand, living in the United Kingdom

'Suki Gokal's book inspires deep reflection, encouraging us to pause, shift our perspective and embrace the wholeness we are meant to embody.'
— **Jennifer K. Hill**, from United States of America, living in Portugal

'Perhaps Sukaiyna's greatest strength has been her ability to listen, without judgement, calmly allowing us to see ourselves in her mirror, as she gently guides us with words of encouragement and enlightenment and reminds us of those things that we innately know make us better citizens of the world.'
— **Phil Redpath**, world traveler, currently living in New Zealand

'This book has been a gift to my soul. Every word felt like you were reading my heart, capturing thoughts I couldn't express. Despite our different worlds, your values and wisdom deeply resonate with me. You've inspired me to grow, and I truly believe this book can change lives.'
— **Juliana Adorno**, from Brazil, living in New York

'"We are products of our decisions, not of our circumstances": *The Human TOUCH* is a profound guide to self-reflection and growth. Sukaiyna Gokal's insights empower readers to embrace harmony, nurture inner peace and inspire meaningful connections with ourselves and others. A roadmap for authentic living.'
  — **Dimitris Orfanidis**, from Greece and Bulgaria, living in Europe, Asia and the Middle East

'A beautifully written resource for those seeking personal growth and deeper understanding of self. The book offers practical tools and poses deep questions, reflecting on our various roles in life. I found myself pausing often to soak in the insights. Intelligent and encouraging toward openness and tolerance. Grab the book, your future self will thank you!'
  — **Tarja Arvela-Yilmaz**, from Finland, living in the United Arab Emirates

'Sukaiyna touches upon the human mindset and segments it into pieces emphasising on ways whereby we can actually find a mechanism of mental peace and harmony. The book also shows means how a personality can be revamped to make a person better, and be relieved from the hardships of fixated preconceived notions. Very unique!'
  — **Waleed Morshed**, Dhaka, Bangladesh

'*The Human TOUCH* is a book that manages to tastefully blend story telling with self-reflection. Sukaiyna Gokal simplifies many complex ideas and helps direct the reader towards an important introspection. This book is a must-read for people looking to align the heart, mind and soul.'
— ***Aman Karim***, **from Canada and France, living in Dubai United Arab Emirates**

'This book is a powerful guide to aligning your heart, body, soul and mind. It awakens your intuition, inviting you to move beyond overthinking and simply feel. What I love most is that it not only offers deep wisdom, but also practical tools to surrender, quiet your inner critic and release judgment.'
— **Veronique Smans**, Belgium

'Sukaiyna Gokal's The *Human TOUCH* is an accessible guide to self-discovery and personal growth. It introduces TOUCH—tolerance, openness, unity, collaboration and harmony—as a framework for introspection and transformation. I found it an easy way to encourage understanding of oneself and accepting others.'
— **Aaditya Sarna**, from India, living in Dubai United Arab Emirates

'*The Human TOUCH* is a deeply reflective and empowering journey into self-awareness, empathy and transformation. This book provides practical

tools for personal growth and inspires readers to connect with themselves and others at a deeper level.'
— **Sarah Habib**, from Pakistan, living in Singapore

'*The Human TOUCH* is a true invitation to introspection and personal transformation. Through heartfelt wisdom and touching humanity, this book explores tolerance, love and unity, guiding us toward a more harmonious life. An essential guide to illuminate our paths.'
— **Patrick Huguenin**, Switzerland

'A masterful guide to rediscovering your authentic self. *The Human TOUCH* is a delicate yet profound mirror that captures the beauty of our inner selves.'
— **Flordeliza Follante**, from Philippines, living in Dubai, United Arab Emirates

'I have followed Sukaiyna Gokal's inspiring work for some years now. *The Human TOUCH* is written in a universal language. It feels as though it is written from her soul. It is truly a necessary journey of discovery every seeker must traverse for a qualitative understanding of life.'
— **Haroon NoorMohammed**, Pretoria, South Africa

'In order to love someone, you must first love yourself. In an effortless and natural way, *The Human*

TOUCH reveals how relationships are mirrors, and helps you flow through your different life events and challenges. It is an enriching journey of unconditional love that makes it safe for us to be ourselves.'
— **Eléonore Lambilliotte**, from Belgium living in Paris, France

'I've witnessed the successful, practical application of personal enrichment methods shared within *The Human TOUCH*. It's a fascinating work and the author's genuine care and innovative approach to helping people overcome deep challenges radiate throughout. Within its pages, the reader is invited into Garden of Ayden – a place that welcomes all cultural backgrounds and where the seeds of enlightenment flourish, enabling unique healing journeys.'
— **Michael Witbraad**, from the Bahamas, living in Angola

'Sukaiyna Gokal's book *The Human TOUCH* masterfully guides readers through transformative self-discovery, urging us to embrace inner truths and shared experiences for personal and collective growth. A truly enlightening read.'
— **Fabien Fryns**, from Belgium living in Dubai, United Arab Emirates

'*The Human TOUCH* provided me with an intuitive roadmap to unravel inner trauma and guide a pathway into a more emotionally enriched life.

I believe the Garden of Ayden offers an intuitive mode of self-reflection to disentangle hidden and overlooked toxic reflexes. I hope this book will be thought of as a third "eye" guide to happiness in an ever-challenging world.'

— **Zygi Balinski**, from Jersey, living across Europe

'Sukaiyna Gokal's *The Human TOUCH* is an inspirational read that provides an equally profound and practical framework for cultivating deeper connections, most interestingly, with oneself. Concisely capturing over a decade of her work from Garden of Ayden, Gokal's gentle and insightful observations in elegant prose make the book a joy to consume.'

— **Holley Chant**, United States of America

'*The Human TOUCH* is an incredible self-journey Suki is taking you on, allowing you to gain a deeper and profound understanding of not only yourself but also your surroundings – suddenly everything makes sense, and you are ready to march forward with a clear vision.'

— **Sahag Arslanian**, Armenian from Belgium, living in Hong Kong

'*The Human TOUCH* is a luminous work that gently and deeply invites introspection. This book offers an accessible and engaging methodology for exploring limiting beliefs, guiding readers step by step toward a rewarding personal transformation. An inspiring and interactive read that brilliantly combines reflection and action.'

— **Sébastien Vieljeux**, from Switzerland, living in United Arab Emirates

'In the labyrinth that is our life, *The Human TOUCH* is the thread of Ariadne that helps us discover ourselves along our journey, find our way when we are lost and ultimately guides us to find and flourish throughout our lives.'

— **Tania N Tourbier**, from Lebanon, living in Dubai, United Arab Emirates

'*The Human TOUCH* by Sukaiyna Gokal is a brilliant, step by step blueprint which guides readers through the essential role that empathy, compassion and authentic relationships play in nurturing self-love, inner peace and a healthier global community.'

— **Rami Tabiaat**, Lebanese-American, living in Oman

Resources

Self-reflective tools

1.1: The Four Goals of Garden of Ayden,
www.gardenofayden.com/
11thefourgoalsofgardenofayden

1.2: Series of Thought Reflective Questions,
www.gardenofayden.com/
12seriesofthoughtreflectivequestions

1.3: How Free Are You?,
www.gardenofayden.com/
13howfreeareyou

2.1: Forgiveness Exercise,
www.gardenofayden.com/
21forgivenessexercise

2.2: The Reason Why Self-Assessment,
www.gardenofayden.com/
22thereasonwhyself-assessment

2.3: The Rules,
www.gardenofayden.com/23therules

3.1: Impact of My Behaviour on Others,
www.gardenofayden.com/
31impactofmybehaviouronothers

3.2: Personality Tests,
www.gardenofayden.com/
32personalitytests

3.3: The Journey,
www.gardenofayden.com/33thejourney

4.1: Practice Makes Perfect,
www.gardenofayden.com/
41practicemakesperfect

RESOURCES

4.2: Triggers,
www.gardenofayden.com/42triggers

4.3: Battles Worth Fighting For,
www.gardenofayden.com/
43battlesworthfightingfor

5.1: Communication Style,
www.gardenofayden.com/
51communicationstyle

5.2: Action Vs Intention,
www.gardenofayden.com/
52actionvsintention

5.3: Clearing the Heart,
www.gardenofayden.
com/53clearingtheheart

6.1: Trust, www.gardenofayden.com/
61trust

6.2: A Measuring Guide,
www.gardenofayden.com/
62ameasuringguide

The Muse Journal

www.gardenofayden.com/the-muse

Garden of Ayden Meditation

www.gardenofayden.com/meditation

Garden of Ayden Radio Playlist

https://open.spotify.com/playlist/7IJtzTKeIxQHszteuXPVm1?si=1G9A2mawRC2Od3Gz1lf3dg

Acknowledgements

I would like to express tremendous gratitude to every single person that has crossed my path through life. We all gain so much from each encounter, experience and epiphany.

Irrespective of whether we believe it or not, it remains true, nonetheless. Nothing is to be discounted in this beautiful and fragile journey of a precious life.

I sincerely hope that my words may touch the most blasé and hardheaded among us on our planet of eight billion plus people today.

It may sound unusual to say the above, however the following statement is humbly to be absorbed and remembered:

Our biggest learnings and growth spurts come from our most painful and difficult experiences. This is why I feel grateful for the most challenging moments as much as, if not more, than for those who are responsible for my bliss. I constantly remind myself that my bliss would not have been possible without all the heartache and horror. The people who we feel may have cracked us open, tormented us, scarred us, bruised us or shattered our dreams are in fact a blessing and the tool from which brings flight to our wings and healing to our expansive hearts.

We know now that our path deserved a grace they could not fulfil or live up to – a warmth and kindness they were incapable of – so should we or had we stayed in undeserving situations we are neglecting not only ourselves but unfairly jeopardising and limiting our own potential. Most importantly, we never allow anyone's words, actions or attitudes to define how we perceive ourselves or our capacity to grow to our highest and best, however we may perceive it.

My Captain, God bless his soul, used to say '*Pour vivre heureux, vivons cachés*', which literally means 'to live happily, live hidden'. This is the exact opposite of the tendency in our world today and while with purpose, for the sake of impact and healing, we may share our work, I believe that peace is truly found within the gemstones of our tranquil garden.

Angels of my physical world, you know who you are. Bless.

The Author

Sukaiyna identifies as an omnist, viewing herself as a child of the universe rather than defining herself by any specific origin or country of birth. She believes that our journeys of growth and self-realisation are not bound by where we are born or where we die, as we all ultimately share the same origin and destination.

For Sukaiyna, her religion is humanity first, and her nationality is being human, embodying a universal love and compassion that transcends borders. She is dedicated to fostering a global community of care and understanding, where everyone is seen, heard and valued equally.

Sukaiyna's journey, amidst both challenges and comfort, inspired her to embark on a path of self-discovery. She believes that true luxury lies in nurturing our inner selves – our mental, emotional and spiritual growth – for a peaceful life, not just for ourselves but also for our future generations.

In 2012, Sukaiyna founded Garden of Ayden, influenced by her studies in psychology as well as eclectic cultural and religious teachings. This platform, which so far is in twenty-eight languages, embodies universal values aimed at empowering individuals to navigate life's obstacles with diligence, dignity and determination.

Sukaiyna maintains a global perspective in her approach, having travelled, lived and worked across the globe, aided by the knowledge of eight languages.

Her purpose, through Garden of Ayden, is to establish a global common language of ethics that is understood by all. She personally guides individuals and families towards being balanced and empowered, while being centred in a mindset of peace and prosperity.

🌐 www.gardenofayden.com

www.ingramcontent.com/pod-product-compliance
Lightning Source LLC
Chambersburg PA
CBHW011957150426
43200CB00018B/2927